Police on Patrol:
The Other Side of the Story

by Linda Kleinschmidt

AJ Publishing, Hartford, Connecticut

Illustrations by Jack Egan
Edited by Deena Quilty
Graphic design by Deena Quilty

Police on Patrol:
The Other Side of the Story

Published by AJ Publishing, PO Box 4277, Hartford, CT 06147-4277

All rights reserved. No part of this book may be reproduced or transmitted in any form or by any means, electronic or mechanical, including photocopying, recording or by any information storage and retrieval system without written permission from the author, except for the inclusion of brief quotations in a review.

copyright © 1996 by Linda Kleinschmidt

First printing: January 1996

Second printing: September 1996

Third printing: September 1997

ACKNOWLEDGMENT

I'd like to thank the hundreds of law enforcement officers, both Municipal and State Police for allowing me to interview them on a one to one basis, as well as those which submitted their written responses to the questionnaire. By nature and occupation, officers in general are very cautious and suspicious individuals. I am very pleased the officers trusted me enough to speak with me very candidly, although it did take a considerable amount of time and effort on my part to gain their trust and confidence. The responding chiefs, supervisors, troopers and patrolmen and women will see through *On Patrol: The Other Side of the Story* that they made a correct judgment in trusting in me to show the "uninformed" public, what their daily activities entail.

Many of the officers gave up their lunch and dinner breaks, spoke with me after their shifts and some even on their days off. I'm grateful to the superior officers which allowed me the opportunity to ride with a number of patrolmen on their shifts and see first hand what they encounter on a day to day basis. Day or night, afternoon or evening, I always found an officer willing to give me their time and insights.

The support and encouragement I received from Connecticut's law enforcement community was overwhelming. Thanks to everyone.

Special thanks to:

    Connecticut Police Chief's Association

    Chief Leroy Bangham, Farmington Police

    Chief Patrick Hedge, Stonington Police

    Master Sgt. Scott O'Mara, CT State Police

    Col. Joseph S. Perry, Commanding Officer, Retired - CT State Police

    Chief Robert A. Williams, Suffield Police

and every officer I interviewed.

"ROLL CALL"

Police Code of Ethics iv

Connecticut State Police Code of Honor v

Introduction 1

Excuses 5

Routine Calls? 25

Off Duty Reactions 67

Most Bothersome Criminal Acts 73

Create Your Own Law 79

Accidents and Incidents 87

Off the Clock Difficulties 101

Crime Prevention 109

Public Perception 115

Sounding Board 123

Commentary

    Anonymous Police Officer —"Frustration" 134

    Col. Joseph S. Perry, Retired —"Who Will Wear the Badge?" 138

    Chief Patrick Hedge—"Career Choice" 140

    Chief Robert A. Williams—"Fear" 142

    Chief Leroy Bangham—"Controversy" 144

Municipal Police Directory 145

State Police Directory 153

Police Code of Ethics

As a law enforcement officer, my fundamental duty is to serve mankind; to safeguard lives and property; to protect the innocent against deception, the weak against oppression or intimidation, and the peaceful against violence or disorder; and to respect the Constitutional rights of all men to liberty, equality and justice.

I will keep my private life unsullied as an example to all; maintain courageous calm in the face of danger, scorn, or ridicule; develop self-restraint; and be constantly mindful of the welfare of others. Honest in thought and deed in both my person and official life, I will be exemplary in obeying the laws of the land and the regulations of my department. Whatever I see or hear of a confidential nature or -that is confided to me in my official capacity will be kept ever secret unless revelation is necessary in the performance of my duty.

I will never act officiously or permit personal feelings, prejudices, animosities, or friendships to influence my decisions. With no compromise for crime and with relentless prosecution of criminals, I will enforce the law courteously and appropriately without fear or favor, malice or ill will, never employing unnecessary force or violence and never accepting gratuities.

I recognize the badge of my office as a symbol of public faith, and I accept it as a public trust to be held so long as I am true to the ethics of the police service. I will constantly strive to achieve these objectives and ideals, dedicating myself before God to my chosen profession . . . law enforcement.

The code of ethics adopted by the International Association of Chiefs of Police in 1957.

Connecticut State Trooper's Code of Honor

I am a Connecticut State Trooper - a soldier of the law. To me is entrusted the honor of the Department.

I will serve the State of Connecticut honestly and faithfully and, if need be, lay down my life as others have done rather than swerve from the path of duty.

I will be loyal to my superiors, obey the law and enforce the law without discrimination as to class, color, creed or condition and without Fear of favor.

I will help those in danger or distress, and at all times conduct myself so as to uphold the honor of the Department.

INTRODUCTION

First of all, I am *not* a police officer, nor am I employed by any law enforcement agency. Several of my friends are Hartford Police Officers. Over the years, I've listened to them talk of the problems they've encountered while on duty. At times it seemed to them that risking their lives while arresting drug dealers, child molesters, car thieves, murder suspects and responding to domestic violence calls, that it all amounts to a drop in the bucket of progress. They see the same faces over and over again. They arrest the perpetrators and they're back out on the street committing the same offense, sometimes even in the same day.

It became apparent to me that the public's view and perception of a police officer and his or her job is actually very distorted. The only contact most citizens have with the law are traffic violations. People generally believe what they see on television. They don't understand what an officer does, or what their daily activities entail.

I decided to write this book for another reason, to point out that only a few officers violate our public trust. Every time an officer commits a crime, it reflects on all police, not only in Connecticut, but across the country. There are many thousands of law enforcement officers; it only takes a few to tarnish the image of the many. The "bad officers" who violate the public trust cause "good officers" to be held accountable for the few.

This book is written for the uninformed. Hopefully, when you're done reading this book, you'll have a better understanding about who the police are and what they do for all of us. Possibly you'll get more involved in the issues affecting your own community and stop blaming the officer(s) for any tickets you might be issued.

On Patrol: The Other Side of the Story is an accumulation of officers' responses to eleven questions:

(1) What was the most creative excuse used by a motorist who had just committed a moving violation?

(2) What was the strangest "call" you were ever summoned to?

(3) What was the most bizarre accident you were ever called to?

(4) What was the most unbelievable incident you ever witnessed?

Introduction

(5) When off duty, how do people react when they find out that you're an officer?

(6) What criminal act bothers you the most?

(7) If you could create a law that would be enforced, what would it be? (No plea bargaining.)

(8) If you were given the opportunity to speak to the public concerning crime and/or prevention of crime, what would be your message?

(9) Is it difficult to leave your job out of your personal/home life when you're off the clock?

(10) What do you dislike the most of the public's perception of you and your job?

(11) What was the funniest excuse used by someone you arrested on why they committed the crime(s)?

Also included are commentaries of three Police Chiefs, the Commander of the State Police, as well as an anonymous Police Officer, who were kind enough to contribute to the book. Many officers didn't wish to have their names revealed. To respect this request, all the stories and comments are anonymous. Some encounters are amusing, many are incredible and some are down right bizarre. The stories are true and are told from their hearts.

My research in visiting police departments, riding along on shifts, interviewing police officers and witnessing arrests, has been a real eye opener. I've changed. Perhaps, it was having suicides described to me in detail, seeing officers with tears in their eyes and voices cracking, telling me about children who had been tortured and dismembered in senseless or intentional auto accidents. There wasn't a specific incident. It was the accumulative effect of all of them. My personal opinion about society and what needs to be changed has only become stronger as a consequence of writing and researching this book.

Crime is a universal problem. People need to get involved to stop it. They need to take responsibility for their own actions and stop putting the blame elsewhere. Children learn by example and many people are setting some very bad examples for our younger generations.

We must make our prisons "prisons," and not country clubs. Many people do not realize that we actually pay unemployment to prisoners in some jails! The legal system is failing because we fail to enforce the sentences on those that have broken the law.

Introduction

Too many people are worried about the Constitutional Rights of the criminals, at the expense of the taxpayers and the victims. Jail is meant to be a punishment, often times it's not. It's up to each one of us to see that criminals are held accountable for their crimes. A person who commits a crime should lose his rights, not gain rights and privileges once behind bars.

The police are meant to serve and protect, but many times their work is wasted. They do their job and arrest those which are deemed guilty of a crime or breaking the law; yet we blame the police if we see the criminal out on the street again the same afternoon. It's not the police; it's our legal system and laws. Give the officers a break. Help provide them with information so they can solve the crimes or apprehend the suspects. Don't think that someone else will get involved. You need to get involved.

Introduction

EXCUSES

It's amazing the excuses people use when they're stopped for motor vehicle violations, at the scene of accidents, when caught driving while under the influence, stealing, and testify in domestic disputes. People fail to realize there are few new stories. Police listen to stories all day long, some are funny, few are legitimate, but most are just plain stupid.

Before they approach, an officer already knows you're going to try and get out of the ticket by offering an excuse. Remember, the officer is doing his job. Don't blame him for issuing you a ticket which may result in higher insurance premiums or your losing your license. He didn't make you speed or drive while intoxicated. You did. You broke the law and the officer is just enforcing the law, which by the way, we as American citizens have created in our democratic society. The officer is there to protect the safety of the public. You are the public.

This chapter deals with just a few of the excuses our Connecticut Law Enforcement Officers have heard. You might even recognize your own excuse(s). I did.

I stopped a woman for running a stop sign. She said that she thought a stop sign with a white border was optional after 7 P.M.

"I couldn't stop officer, the gas pedal got stuck."

One day while running radar, I stopped a woman for speeding. Her excuse: She just found out that her sister was anorexic and she needed to get home in a hurry.

Excuses

We arrested these kids for buying alcohol under age. The parent's response was: "I didn't know that package stores sold liquor. I thought they only sold beer."

A woman driving all over the road was stopped for reckless driving. The story was, her bra had become unhooked and she was attempting to hook it up.

A woman came to the police station to file a complaint. When charged, she said, "You can't arrest me because I'm the one making the complaint." She then proceeded to attack the arresting officer.

We confronted a woman who had shoplifted Midol. She insisted that it was that time of the month and she really needed it.

I arrested a husband for assaulting his wife. He said, "Officer, I just snapped. I was tired of coming home every single night and finding my wife in bed with my uncle."

I stopped a woman for speeding and told her I caught her on radar. She got very upset and yelled, "I hate when I get my picture taken and I haven't combed my hair properly."

Excuses

A man: "Yellow means to speed up, which I did. I thought I could make it, but I guess my timing was off."

When I arrived at the scene of a one car accident, I found the driver intoxicated. He insisted he wasn't the driver. It was his dog.

"I'm sorry officer, I was just going too fast to stop for the light."

I pulled this young woman over for speeding. She said, "I just caught my fianceé cheating."

Excuses

"I didn't know my license was suspended," is a normal response.

Some people actually start yelling when given a ticket. "You ruined my day." "It's your fault that I'm going to lose my license." I didn't make them speed but they blame me.

The guy said he was speeding because he had on new shoes and couldn't feel the pedal because they weren't broken in yet.

I stopped her for speeding and she had an interesting excuse: "Officer, the play was so bad that I had to get away from the theater as fast as I possibly could."

I stopped this woman in an Austin Healy for speeding. As I approached, I saw that she was wearing a fishnet dress and nothing else. She didn't need to give me a reason for speeding. I just gave her a verbal warning and sent her on her way as quickly as I could.

"I was speeding, Officer, because my daughter is late for her driving instruction."

She told me that I couldn't give her a ticket because she was a resident of the town and tickets were only for 'nonresidents.

I pulled this woman over for speeding. She wasn't wearing anything from the waist down except for a large bandage. She said she was on her way to pick up her medication and the reason she wasn't wearing anything down there was because the cool air from the vents felt good.

A flip of the hair as you approach is a pretty good indication that the blouse will be unbuttoned or the dress pulled up. I still give them tickets, as quickly as possible.

I stopped this woman for speeding. She said she was on the way to the hospital, with internal bleeding. I let her go, but decided to follow her to the emergency room. I found her just sitting there in her car. So I went over to help her, whereupon, she said she had a confession to make. She had lied, there was nothing wrong. She hadn't expected me to follow her to the hospital. She was an attorney. I gave her a ticket.

When I stopped the motorist, he proceeded to tell me he was good friends with Officer "So and So," and that the officer told him to use his name if he was ever stopped. He was using my name. I gave him a ticket.

She didn't stop for the red light. When I pulled her over, she said that if she stopped, her car would stall, so she didn't stop for the red light. I pointed out to her that she was now stopped, and her car was still running.

Excuses

There seems to be no creative excuse for failure to have emissions testing done. They're always planning on doing it tomorrow.

I pulled her over for DUI, and the car following also pulled over. When questioned, the second motorist said her friend was driving the car that I'd stopped. I asked her if she knew that her friend was drunk. She said, "Yes, that's why I'm following her home."

An elderly woman ran a stop sign and I pulled her over. She said she was sorry and wouldn't do it again then proceeded to drive away. I yelled and ran after her. I told her I had to give her a ticket. She started to cry and told me that I couldn't give her a ticket, she's never gotten one before and it would spoil her record. It took me awhile to calm her down before I could write the ticket.

I had heard about this from other officers, but I thought they were just kidding, until it happened to me. One night on the late shift I pulled a woman over for speeding. As I approached the window, she was lifting up her skirt. Her face turned beat red when she noticed that I was a female officer.

A woman told me she was speeding because she was late for court; she had gotten a ticket for speeding last month

Excuses

I pulled a man over for running a stop sign. He claimed he hadn't seen it. I suggested that he get his eyes checked immediately. The stop sign was huge. It was one of the oversized ones that you couldn't miss with normal sight.

"The only explanation, officer, is 'spontaneous acceleration.' This car has a mind of it's own."

A man checked into a hotel, then proceeded to rob it. This case was easy to solve. He'd registered under his own name when checking in and went back to his room after the robbery. His excuse: he needed money to pay for another night.

I stopped this man for speeding and DUI. He refused to give me his license until I showed him that I had a license to run the radar. I pointed to my badge and wrote out the ticket.

Excuses

This woman whose husband is in politics, hits a vehicle and then drives off. We tracked her down. She said she had a hair appointment and couldn't wait especially since her hair was more important than stopping for a minor accident.

A woman was issued a ticket early one morning for parking in a "No Parking" zone. The woman wrote to the newspaper complaining that police have better things to do than to ticket law abiding citizens. A reader responded to her letter saying she'd give the police less to do if she didn't park in a "No Parking" zone to begin with.

I pulled this guy over for exceeding the speed limit. He said that his wife had a baby yesterday and he was rushing to the hospital to help her deliver it.

A gentleman said he was speeding to his doctor's office. He was late for a cardiac and stress test.

DUI: This man refused to take the test because he said he was left handed and all the tests were for right handed people.

Excuse for peeling tires: "It's not my car."

Excuses

I pulled a pregnant woman over for speeding who said she was in labor and on the way to the hospital. I pointed it out that the hospital was in the opposite direction. "Oh, I know officer. I want to stop at the store first."

This excuse was used when a person was stopped for running a red light: "I'm color blind and I wasn't sure which light was the red one."

Most people that shoplift have the money to purchase the items they're stealing. Usually the items are stuffed under a baby carriage or in their pockets. Their excuse: They just had overlooked them. An honest mistake. Unfortunately, peer pressure against juveniles has them shoplifting as initiation into the gangs.

When people blow through stop signs, their argument is they stopped or just didn't see the sign.

I actually had someone thank me for the ticket I just gave him. He said his sister has a metal plate in her head because of a car accident she was involved in while speeding.

"I'm looking for a gas station. I didn't want to run out. That's why I was speeding, officer."

Excuses

A man robbed a convenience store at gun point because he wanted a better motel room for him and his girlfriend. He had money but not enough for the type of room she deserved.

When I issued the man a ticket for DUI, he was surprised that I did. He was handicapped; he had no legs and the car was rigged up electronically. He responded, "No one ever gives me a ticket." *Wrong*.

They cry. Then when you come back with the ticket, they get very nasty.

Motorcyclists: their glasses just flew off or they parked the bike and someone stole them.

Early one morning I stopped a man for DUI. He said his wife just had their first baby—a son. He then went out and celebrated a little too much. I decided to let him go. I had him park his vehicle and call someone to come and get him. About six months later, while I was riding with a partner, we pulled over the same guy for DUI. He didn't recognize me. He told my partner he was drunk because his wife just had their first baby—a son. He had a little too much to drink. This time he was arrested.

Excuses

"I have to go to the bathroom really bad, officer. I've got diarrhea."

A man caught stealing cigarettes thought the display on the counter was self-service.

"You mean it wasn't yellow? The guy before me made it through."

"Officer, I was just in California and they let you take a left on red.

Excuses

I pulled a husband over for speeding. His wife was screaming at him, and telling me to arrest him. "Give him a ticket. I've told him time and time again to slow down, but does he listen to me? No." I gave him a warning. I felt sorry for him.

I stopped a man for speeding. His excuse was he was rushing to the hospital because his wife was there having their first baby. The poor man was shaking so bad and talking so fast, I figured he had to be telling the truth. Nobody could make themselves look that terrified unless they were about to become a father.

A man broke down in tears with his child in the car. He said between sobs, "I know I shouldn't have been speeding; it sets a bad example for my son."

I stopped a woman for speeding. She said she was 4 months pregnant and was in labor. Her water had broken and she was en route to the hospital.

When I've stopped females for speeding, a frequent excuse is having their periods and they need to get to the ladies room.

At a gas station, a man drove away without paying for the gas. We caught him. He said he just had to get home.

Excuses

I pulled over an intoxicated motorist. I asked him how much he had to drink. I received an honest answer, "More than I'd care to tell you, officer."

The woman I stopped for a violation had hiked up her skirt. I went to the cruiser to write up the ticket. When I came back with the summons, the skirt was down and she had an incredibly nasty attitude.

I stopped a woman for speeding; she said her child had to go to the bathroom. The kid was actually shaking in the back seat of the car. Whether she told her child to shake like that, I'm not really sure.

Speeding: "I was only going 25 mph not 45 mph, officer.

At 1 A.M. in the morning, I stopped a female for speeding. Her excuse was she had a very high metabolism and without her medication she did everything fast. She was on her way to the pharmacy to pick up a prescription. The woman had given the disease a funny name. It seemed strange to me; she wasn't talking fast and there weren't any open pharmacies in the area at that time of the day.

The "not me" syndrome. DUI's: "I only had a couple of drinks." They stumble out of the car, their back aches and they stay hunched over claiming they're unable to take the test for DUI.

Excuses

One night we arrested 23 guys for soliciting prostitutes. The most frequent comment heard from the men was, "I can't get AIDS from a blow job."

The burglar suspect said he got into the house because the cat showed him how. "It's the cat's fault. He went in first. Arrest him, too."

We stopped a drunk elderly gentleman going 30 mph on the highway. Sparks were flying all over the place. He was driving a car with no tires—only rims.

"What did I do officer?" is a familiar statement whenever I stop someone for a speeding violation.

I stopped a doctor for speeding. He said he was on the way to the hospital for an emergency. A little while later I decided to call the hospital to find out if he really did have an emergency. He didn't. I drove to the hospital and gave him the ticket.

"I thought the light was green, officer."

Excuses

A woman flew past me. When I caught up to her, she said she was in a hurry. Her son had a doctor's appointment and she was running late. I pointed two things out to her: One, she was headed in the wrong direction for her appointment; and two, where was her son?

"I'm rushing to the airport" is a frequent excuse for speeding.

"I thought you could go left on red after stop."

We caught a man stealing money from a parking meter. He said he hadn't used up all his time on the meter and wanted a refund.

Excuses

Shoplifting: We picked up a rather large man for shoplifting a bra and girdle. He said he was tired of seeing his girlfriend droop and the flab turned him off. So he stole the articles for her.

A woman hit a telephone pole in a one car accident. She said there was a spider on the dashboard.

"Officer, that didn't look like a stop sign to me."

I stopped a man going down a one-way street. His response: "I was only going one way."

A woman was speeding and had also ran two red lights. She said she had "PMS and the imbalance of hormones causes her to occasionally drive carelessly."

The lady was speeding home because she had to feed her goldfish.

I gave a gentlemen a ticket for speeding. He said he wouldn't accept it, then proceeded to tear up the ticket and throw it on the ground. I also gave him a ticket for littering.

Excuses

A woman demolished her car. She saw a bee in the car, panicked, let go of the steering wheel and fell to the floor. She forgot she was driving the car.

The man was rushing home. The pizza he bought was getting cold. He said, "It's not my fault for speeding. If the pizza place delivered, I never would have been driving the car in the first place."

I stopped a motorist for speeding. The man said he had to get home before his license expired.

Excuses

A motorist put their blinker on and moved into my lane, almost hitting my cruiser. They thought they had the right of way once they put their signal on.

I pulled over a woman driving a van for speeding. She absolutely refused to roll down her window. "How do I know you're a real police officer?" I showed her my ID and badge. "It could be fake." I pointed out my marked cruiser. She then said, "It could be stolen." I showed her my radio. She still didn't believe me. Apparently, she watched an episode of Oprah Winfrey warning against people impersonating police officers. My supervisor showed up. Finally, she rolled down her window a crack so she could give me her license, registration and insurance card. I then slipped everything back through the crack in the window, including her summons.

Around 1 o'clock in the afternoon, I issued a ticket for parking in a handicapped parking space. A man came running down the street after me. He said, with the ticket in his hand, "But officer, it's after 12 o'clock. After 12 it's no longer a Handicapped Parking space."

Whenever I stop attorneys for a moving violation, they usually hand me their business card along with their license and registration. They think that I won't give them a ticket because of their profession. Wrong.

Excuses

I stopped a very attractive blond for speeding. I gave her a summons. She asked while flashing a smile, "What can I do about this ticket, officer?" I told her she had two choices. One, she could plead 'not guilty' or two, she could pay the fine. Boy, did she turn ugly.

I stopped this woman for reckless driving; she was all over the road. When I pulled her over, she jumped out of the car, screaming. Apparently, there was a bee in the car and she was allergic to bees.

The woman said her ice cream was melting and needed to get home in a hurry before it stained the seat. That's why she was speeding.

"Officer, please don't give me a ticket. I borrowed the car without permission and I wanted to get it back before it was missed."

"I left the scene of the accident because I had to go and pay my insurance premium, officer."

When I stopped a man for speeding, he said he was losing the reception on his car phone and needed to get closer to another tower.

23

Excuses

ROUTINE CALLS?

This chapter deals with different calls and incidents that were either witnessed by the officers or ones they were summoned to investigate. It encompasses a very broad spectrum, to show that the police encounter many different and unusual situations. Their job is not to just stop people for speeding or DUI.

Law enforcement officers see so much when they're out patrolling; most people would be astonished. Many people have a tendency to believe all the crimes and disturbances are made public. This is often not the case, especially in incidents where no arrest is made.

When you get upset at an officer for issuing you a ticket for speeding and you don't have your child in a car seat, you may feel he overreacted or was rude to you. What you may not realize is that he may have just come from arresting a man for sexually assaulting a 14 month old baby, who is now in the hospital in intensive care. Then there you are, failing to protect your child in a car seat. He or she may have just come from a serious car accident where people either died or were maimed for life. Your speeding or reckless driving may seem trivial to you, but what officers witness daily are often tragic consequences. There are so many variables which we, as citizens, don't see.

Some of the incidents you'll find to be stated in a very basic fashion, without graphic detail. I've left it up to you, the reader, to visualize the consequences. Most of the more gruesome cases were described to me in detail. I feel the officers don't need to see them graphically in print, when it's hard enough for them to try and forget the suicides, murders, dismemberments, violence, accidents and abuses they encounter almost daily in their jobs.

> At the scene of a murder, we found the suspect had killed his gay lover. The victim's penis had been severed off. We located the severed appendage in a frying pan on the kitchen stove. It had been cooked and a bite had been taken out of it. It was disgusting.

Routine Calls?

Late one evening, I was asked to investigate the sighting of a young girl seen in the window of an old boarded up house. The house hadn't been lived in for years. There was no electricity. When I arrived, I could see on the second floor a light on and a little girl standing in the window. Myself and another officer gained entry to the abandoned house. When we reached the second floor and opened the door, the light was gone and so was the little girl. The room was stone cold. The woman next door told us a nine-year old girl had died years ago in the old house, in the very same room where we'd seen her through the window. Over the years, there have been numerous sightings of the young child. This was my first haunted house experience.

While patrolling a local street, I noticed a woman parked on the side of the road, sitting in the passenger seat. She acted oddly—erratically turning her head and looking around. I went around the block again to see if she needed help. Now she had her head leaning on the headrest. As I approached the vehicle., I noticed a man on the floor, ah . . . taking care of her sexual needs.

A drunk woman called us to report a possible break-in. When we arrived, she was in a night gown. It was a false alarm. All she wanted was company.

Sometimes people think we're veterinarians. On several occasions I've been called to separate two dogs mating which had gotten stuck together. "What are we supposed to do, carry K-Y in our glove compartment? Please, next time, call a vet."

Routine Calls?

This is an instance where it would have been nice if the neighbors had gotten involved a week or so earlier. They knew it was strange they hadn't seen their elderly neighbor for several days. The neighbors waited eleven days before calling and reporting her absence to us. When we arrived at the elderly woman's residence, we found her dead. The coroner said she died of natural causes and had been dead for about a week and a half. The weather outside had also been in the nineties. I can't even describe to you the odor which comes from a deceased person, but it's something that once you've smelled it, you'll never forget it.

I came across a couple parking in their car. When I approached the window, I could see the woman performing oral sex on the man. He asked me to wait until she was done.

I went to a "call" concerning an animal locked in a trunk. A passerby phoned us to let us know she had heard a lot of commotion in the parked vehicle. A local animal trainer left the bear in the truck while he went shopping; the animal was getting restless.

We responded to a "medical call." A woman answered the door, in her night gown, covered in blood. We thought she was the injured party. She wasn't; it was her husband. Apparently, they were heavily engaged in oral sex and the wife got a little carried away in the heat of passion, accidentally biting almost completely off her husband's penis. It was hanging on by only a thread. As the husband was being placed in the ambulance, he was pleading with us not to arrest his wife, it wasn't her fault.

Routine Calls?

We received a call of a snake in a woman's garage. When we opened the door, we found, much to our surprise, a nine-foot Python and not a garter snake as we had expected. We needed a slightly larger cage than what we had brought.

A doctor alerted us to the fact that one of his patients had been eight months pregnant—now she wasn't. The woman went to see him on an emergency call because she was bleeding. The woman then insisted she was never pregnant. We rushed to her apartment and searched for the baby. After searching for some time, we opened the cabinet where the garbage was stored. Inside the trash was another garbage bag, tied in a knot. When we lifted it out of the garbage, we found the baby—dead. We later found out the baby had died less than 20 minutes before we found her. How can people do something like this to an innocent baby? It's more than upsetting.

Routine Calls?

We were summoned to a disturbance in an apartment building. The neighbors had reported a woman's screams coming from one of the apartments. We knocked on the door. A man with a towel wrapped around his waist greeted us at the door. Apparently, he and his female companion were having a very loud sexual encounter.

We received a "medical call" from a husband saying his diabetic wife was dead on the bathroom floor. I spoke to the husband in the living room, while the other officer, who had just watched the movie—Friday the 13th—the night before, went to check on the woman. Just as he grabbed the woman's wrist, she sat up. The other officer was scared almost half to death. She's still alive today.

I was out on patrol when I heard muffled yells for help. I located a man, wearing only his underwear, stuck in a chimney. The man had been attempting to gain entry to the house he'd intended to rob. He threw his clothes down the chimney and planned on sliding down after them. But he got stuck.

A guy wanted us to arrest another man for stealing his cocaine. "It cost me money and I want the money from him. He won't pay me, so I want him arrested." Is that wild or what?

Routine Calls?

We got a call from a woman that two people were breaking into her house. She lived on the first floor. The woman stayed on the line and told us the perpetrators were in the kitchen. We surrounded the house and then the phone line went dead. We immediately entered through the back door, fearing for the woman's safety—only to find there wasn't anyone in the house to begin with. She lied.

I startled this couple who were parking one night. They got so scared when I pulled up, they both jumped out of the car—naked.

There was a call of a robbery in progress, just as we were in the middle of a shift change. When we jumped into the cruiser, a third officer also hopped into the back seat of the car. You can't open the back door from the inside. As we were in pursuit, he kept telling us not to forget to open the door when the foot chase starts. Well, when the foot chase started, in the commotion, we forgot to let him out. The other officer and I took off after the suspect, as soon as the car came to a stop. We pursued the suspect over a fence, right through the backyard of a house with a wedding reception in progress. I'm sure it added a little more to their wedding video seeing a police chase. When we finally apprehended the suspect and brought him back to the cruiser, we noticed our other fellow officer sitting in the back of the cruiser with a crowd of people around the car. Boy, was he not a happy camper.

A 100,000-pound construction beam crushed a man who was holding the rope when the cable broke. He was killed instantly. It took almost four hours to lift the beam off of him. It was hot out . . . it was awful . . .

Routine Calls?

A 400-pound elderly man was stuck in a bath tub. He was squished up like an accordion. Apparently, he'd slipped on the rug and fell into the tub with his feet dangling out over the edge. His wife, in trying to be helpful, let the water out of the tub. That made it worse. The other officer and I couldn't get him out of the tub. He was really stuck. We had to call for backup. I really felt sorry for the old man. He was more embarrassed than anything, especially since one of the responding officers was a woman.

A woman called the police department and told us that she had been getting harassing phone calls and that at the time she was phoning us, someone was in the house. When we got there, she opened the door and invited us in. That's when we noticed the ax in her hands. She started asking us if we heard the voices. She asked, "Can't you hear them?" She then decided we weren't police officers. "You're not the police! You're working with him!" She said that "he," the voice, wanted to feel her, etc. . . . We were able to get the ax out of her hands, then we brought her in for a psychiatric evaluation.

We received a report from the Navy that one of their sailors was missing. We decided to call in a psychic to help us locate the missing person. He was last seen driving in the vicinity of the river. The psychic said the man was in the water. Divers searched all day, but turned up nothing. On the second day, the psychic still insisted the sailor was in the water. He pointed to where, the day before, the ferry had been docked. We sent in the diver team again. Sure enough, we found the sailor and car, in the water. The ferry had been floating over the man and car the day before.

Routine Calls?

Another officer and I were called to a Domestic Disturbance. The parties involved lived on the third floor of a house which I noted had numerous safety code violations, e.g., rickety stairs and railings. When we arrived at the scene, a very large woman whom we determined to be pretty well intoxicated, had been fighting. Upon arresting her, which she resisted with kicking and screaming, we were finally able to put the cuffs on her. Her resistance didn't end when we had to bring her down the shoddy staircase. The only way we could get he down the stairs was for both of us officers to grab an arm and bring her down backwards. Approximately halfway down the stairs, she decided to have her massive weight go limp. As her heels hit each step, I could hear a thump and hollow clumping. I couldn't understand where that other sound was coming from. When we finally reached the cruiser, which seemed like an eternity, I realized she had a wooden leg.

We arrested a 16 year old boy and in order for us to release him, we needed a parent or guardian's signature. I called his mother and she said she'd be there in awhile; she was in the middle of a cocktail party. Well, I waited almost an hour, then decided to drive the boy back to his house. I arrived at the house with the teenager in handcuffs. Right in front of her guests, I told the woman, "The next time the police ask you to come down to the station and pick up your son, you come to the station—immediately."

Every week we were summoned to the tinfoil lady's residence. She wore a hat made of tinfoil and everything in her house was either tinfoil or aluminum. She explained she needed to be surrounded by tinfoil and aluminum because it was the only way she could make contact with Alpha Centauri. She was finally committed.

Routine Calls?

We received a Domestic Disturbance call. There were three elderly sisters and a brother living at the residence; all were alcoholics and under the influence when we arrived. One sister, the nurse, had just arrived home from work. She wanted her brother arrested because he was under the "Alchofluence of Inchol." It was a crazy scene. The old man started chasing me around the table with a fork in his hand. I guess you'd have to have been there to have appreciated this situation and it's humor.

A man attempted suicide by jumping off a bridge into the river below. But before he jumped, he had stuffed about thirty pounds of rocks from the train tracks into his pockets to help him sink. When he jumped into the water, he still floated. We think he might have changed his mind about killing himself once he hit the water. He told us he wanted to commit suicide because he couldn't do anything right.

An officer radioed the station he was in the pursuit of a suspicious vehicle. The driver refused to pull over and consequently sped up. As the chase crossed the city line, the other police department and the State Police were notified. Over the radio, the pursuing officer was giving a minute by minute account of what was going on and where the suspects were headed. He said the front seat passenger was acting strangely. Even with the cruiser's lights on and the sirens blaring, the car continued on at over 70 mph. The car then pulled into the emergency room with numerous police cars following. The woman was in labor and the husband was oblivious to anything except getting his wife to the hospital. The first officer pursuing still gave the man a ticket.

Routine Calls?

We arrived at the scene of a medical call of an elderly woman in her 80's, having a possible heart attack. She was wearing a hospital bracelet on her wrist. We asked her what the bracelet was for and she said that she'd had a major heart attack, "yesterday". The husband, also in his eighties came over and said, "She just likes to ride in the ambulance." With that, he leaned over her and pushed her in the face as we were administering oxygen. The woman was fine. She did say she liked to travel in ambulances.

This psychopath had asked a woman to marry him. She said "No". He then took a butter knife and cut the head off of his own penis and placed the ring on top of it. The doctors couldn't sew it back on.

We arrested a very large, and very drunk man for beating up his wife. He said she didn't have dinner ready and he felt she deserved to have been beaten.

Myself and two other officers arrived at the scene of a reported Domestic call—loud fight. We knocked on the door and identified ourselves. A man opened it wearing only a bathrobe and an extremely flushed face. Apparently, he and his girlfriend were making love—loudly. When we asked to speak with her, she came to the door in a bathrobe and said that, "If that was a fight, it's the best fight I've ever had." I'm not sure who was more embarrassed, them or us.

Routine Calls?

A man called us to let us know his dog decided to commit suicide by hanging himself. The dog had fallen off the porch and had used his leash as the rope.

A man was protesting the stench in his neighborhood. He decided since he wasn't getting any action from the town, to load up his truck with chicken manure and park it in front of city hall. We had to use gas masks to approach the truck. There wasn't anything in the ordinances saying he was breaking the law. The only thing we could do was issue him a parking ticket once his two hours expired on the meter. He still refused to move his truck. We then decided to get a machine to suck the chicken manure out of the truck. The man brought us to court, wanting his chicken manure returned to him.

Routine Calls?

I received a call of a medical emergency. When I arrived at the home, an eighteen year old boy was sitting on the front steps with a shotgun in his hand. His shoulder had been blown off. I asked him if he was cleaning the gun. He said, "No." He'd been trying to commit suicide, but the gun slipped. All this over the breakup of him and his girlfriend. I let him know that I was there for him if he wanted to talk to me. I called him a few days later at the hospital. We talked. He now has a plastic shoulder. He called several months later to thank me for helping him out. He's got his life back together. This made me feel really good. Not only because I was able to help someone with their problem, but to be thanked for it.

These two people got a little carried away. They couldn't wait to get to a private spot, so they were making love on a picnic table, in broad daylight at a local fast food place.

My first day on the job, I received a call that a crow was attacking a group of children. When I arrived, it was almost like watching an Alfred Hitchcock movie.

People don't realize when we arrest drunks they do get sick in our cruisers and we get to clean up the mess. Worse yet, is the smell when they defecate on themselves in the back seat. Talk about getting the dry heaves.

Routine Calls?

One evening while patrolling down near the river, I saw a large white commercial building on the right, glowing orange. At first, I thought the building was on fire. Driving closer, I noticed that it wasn't. I looked to my left over the river and I saw what I believed to be a UFO. It was hovering over the center of the river. The orange reflection I saw on the building was actually coming from the UFO. I sat there looking at it. There was no noise. Slowly it made itself up the river. I watched it as it started to round the bend, then suddenly it took off in a flash. I turned my cruiser around and headed back towards town. I came across a fellow officer who had also been patrolling in the area. At first, I was afraid to say anything. Then he asked me if I saw it. I knew what he was referring to. We decided not to report what we saw. Later that evening, the sergeant on the desk told us that earlier he had received over 40 phone calls from residents near the river that had sighted a UFO. We then knew we had seen a UFO.

The brother wanted to have sex with his sister. She refused and he tossed her out the second floor window.

The woman's husband came home early from work. Her lover decided to step out on the ledge to avoid being detected. There was no ledge. The man fell nine stories to his death.

We have a resident in town which we refer to as the tinfoil man. He has tinfoil everywhere in the house. He said he needs it because of the gamma rays. The tinfoil scrambles the waves; so does the tinfoil hat he wears around the house.

Routine Calls?

I dislike going to suicides but not as much as failed suicide attempts. This last one, the man only shot off his face, because the gun slipped when he pulled the trigger. The man is deformed for life.

People are sick. A woman went into labor, didn't call for medical assistance, then decided she didn't want the baby and stabs it to death. She said her boyfriend didn't want her to have it anyway.

A woman was giving birth at a residence. I was able to respond before the medical team arrived. This rather large, unmarried girl, living with her parents told me she was just "So . . . surprised." I asked, "Because the baby came so fast?" She said, "No. I didn't even know that I was pregnant. I went in the bathroom because I thought I had gas, and this baby pops out! I was just so . . . surprised!"

We went to the apartment of an elderly gentleman who was hallucinating. He thought there were ghosts coming out of the walls. I went to my cruiser and got a bottle of disinfectant spray. I told him it was anti-ghost spray and I sprayed the area where he thought the ghosts were coming in through. About a week later, he called the department and asked my supervisor where he could get a bottle of the anti-ghost spray so he wouldn't disturb us anymore. I had a little explaining to do.

Routine Calls?

A funny scene we witnessed was back in the seventies when streaking was the fad. At a woman's prep school, running across the lawn, we saw about fifty bare bottoms sprinting from building to building. I miss the seventies.

We received a call from a husband on the 911 line; his wife was after him with a knife. The line went dead. We were dispatched to the residence. The woman had caught her husband in bed with his secretary and the wife had cut the phone line. She was also attempting to cut off her husband's penis. She was very upset, to say the least.

I was sitting in my cruiser running radar in a 30 mph zone, when a car passed me speeding. As the car went by, the horn sounded several quick times. I thought, "This is ridiculous. Here they are speeding and then they call attention to themselves." Immediately, I started in pursuit. I came around the corner and saw smoke. Coming closer to the scene I could see that it was the vehicle that had sped past me, wrapped around a tree. I jumped out of the cruiser. The man had the woman in a choke hold—gun in hand. He then proceeded to fire several shots at me. I called for backup. He told me to leave. I told him I wasn't going anywhere. Just as he dragged the woman around the corner of the house, I noticed a bundle on the ground with what appeared to be a woman's head lying underneath it. Fortunately, upon further investigation, it was only a wig and not someone else in the car that had been decapitated. The SWAT team arrived, and several hours later the man was subdued. The reason he'd only fired those first few shots at me was because the gun had jammed. The woman was the one who, while in the vehicle, had beeped the horn at me. The suspect had kidnapped the victim he was obsessed with from another town several miles away.

Routine Calls?

Two people were found sleeping in a Camaro in broad daylight on the side of a residential street. The woman was in the driver's seat—naked and the man was only wearing his underwear. She got out of the vehicle and refused to put her clothes on. It was February and the temperature was about 20 degrees below zero with the wind chill. There she was, standing next to her car, butt naked. With this job, nothing surprises you.

A dozen or so years ago, we were in the pursuit of a stolen Cadillac on a major highway. The speed we were traveling at ranged from 80 to 90 mph. We radioed ahead to the other officers and, at the time, we were able to do rolling road blocks. At one point during the chase, we got ahead of the stolen vehicle and he rammed into the back of us. The bumpers hooked as he kept pushing our cruiser up the emergency lane. We were stuck together with nowhere to go. The rolling road block prevented us from maneuvering our vehicle in order to separate the cars. Up ahead in the emergency lane was a gas truck broken down. My life started to flash before my eyes. Somehow, the cars became unstuck at the last minute and we missed colliding with the truck. The Cadillac continued on. Later, we found the stolen car but no driver.

We had to bring a few people to the hospital for very strange emergencies. One man had a hatchet stuck in his head, another had to have gerbil removed from his rectum.

This was absolutely amazing. We were scheduled to do a drug raid at a local bar. My partner and I went in first and sat down at the end of the bar. We were wearing our jackets with "Police" written in big bold letters across the back and our weapons and radios were in plain sight. No one even flinched. While we were sitting there, we saw two drug transactions happen right at the bar in front of us. My partner went to the men's room and a man was doing lines of cocaine on the sink. After observing the bar for ten minutes or so, I called for the rest of the officers to come in and make the arrests. As other officers came through the door and yelled, "Police—don't anyone move," everyone seemed surprised. It was strange since we had been sitting there for awhile and no one even paid attention to us.

I approached a car in a secluded area which was known to be a spot for couples parking. I knocked on the window; the woman was engaged in oral sex with her companion. She looked at me, mouth still on his appendage, and motioned with one finger, as if to say, in a minute. I knocked on the window again and she repeated the gesture. Finally, she looked up and swallowed. She told me she had to finish what she had started.

We were summoned to a residence because of a bat in their bedroom. The other senior officer went to the car and returned with a fire extinguisher. I suggested to him that if he'd just open the window and take a broom, you could shush the bat out. He liked his way better. He sprayed the bat, but instead of the extinguisher containing $CO-2$ to freeze the bat, it had a dry chemical powder. (This beautiful bedroom had to be completely remodeled.) I then grabbed a broom and shushed the bat out of the window.

A young kid stole a bus and drove it through the city streets. What was really something is the kid was able to maneuver the bus through a construction site without hitting anyone or anything. A number of blocks away, he'd parked it almost perfectly near the curb—much better than I've seen most bus drivers do.

Routine Calls?

Two lesbian women had just finished having an intimate encounter. They owned a cat, which laid down on the chest of one of the women who was lying on the bed. The other female had grabbed a gun, which she thought wasn't loaded and started to pretend to shoot the cat. Well, there was one bullet in the chamber. The woman blew the head right off the cat and part of it's skull was imbedded in the other woman. We had to bring the cat to the medical examiner to have it tested for rabies. The woman survived; obviously the cat didn't.

My first day on the job I received a call to proceed to a residence—there were chickens on the roof of a car. When I arrived, there were no chickens, no feathers and no complaints. It was definitely odd.

We went to a scene where the father was high on drugs and was dangling his 2 year old out the window by his feet. The man threatened to drop the child from the second floor window, if the police approached. We were finally able to rescue the child. I was definitely scared for the child's life. People are sick. They're even more sick when they're high on drugs.

The mother wanted her daughter, who was in her late twenties, to move out of the house. The daughter refused. She said she wouldn't leave the house because there were demons living upstairs and wanted to stay to protect her mother. The daughter told us to go check upstairs and we'll see the demons. We checked. Nothing. She said, "You were too noise going up the stairs and you scared them away."

Routine Calls?

We arrested a gay man's lover for beating up the other one. As we're going out the door, the victim who had been screaming like a woman, attacked the other officer because we arrested his lover.

A couple in the process of getting a divorce, were involved in a Domestic. The man had defecated on the beige rug in the living room and also urinated in the corner. The couple had not spoken since they started the divorce proceedings. When asked why he had done what he did, the man responded, "She's literally going to get a shitty house." No arrest was made. We had to refer the woman to the Health Department because he hadn't committed a crime.

A man broke up with his girlfriend. She was able to convince him to go to a motel with her for one last tumble in the hay. While there, she started to perform oral sex on him, then she bit it off. Apparently, she wasn't going to let anyone else have "it" if she couldn't.

At a familiar parking spot, The Nature Center, I saw two people in a hatchback. When I got out of the cruiser and approached the window, only the man could be seen in the car. He had pushed the girl into the hatch and closed the top.

I arrived at a "call" and found a man with a bottle of lye tied to a rope, swinging it around his head like he was going to lasso a baby calf, aiming it at the next door neighbor who was pointing a shot gun at the guy with the lye. Before I could even get out of the cruiser, the two had started fighting over the shotgun and had rolled

Routine Calls?

off the cliff at the end of the property—each trying to get control of the gun. Both were finally subdued and arrested. The "lye" guy made bail. It was around 10 P.M. and I was bringing him back to his house. On the way, he asked me to drop him off where there was a lot of light, like the mall. He believed that there was "evil lurking" in the darkness that night. Awhile later, I got a call from another officer patrolling the mall, telling me, "You're not going to believe what I'm looking at!" For some reason, I could believe just about anything. When I got to the mall, there was the "lye" guy—naked—sitting inside a giant hefty bag. He had salt in the bag to ward off the evil spirits. The bag was pulled over the top of his head with only his eyes and the tips of his fingers showing. We brought him to the hospital; he was committed.

The teenage daughter voluntarily had sex with a man and got pregnant. The girl's father found out six months later. He wanted us to arrest the man for rape and getting his daughter pregnant.

We arrested a man for stiffing a cab driver. The suspect was foreign and didn't speak any English. We placed him in the jail cell while we located an interpreter. While in the cell, he not only flooded the toilet, but also started to throw feces at the other prisoners. They started to complain. I don't blame them. We finally located an interpreter; the man was instructed to clean up his mess. He did.

When we arrived at a Domestic, everything in the house was broken. Windows, mirrors, chairs, plates. The husband and wife had literally beaten the crap out of each other. As we separated the two, we could see that the woman's shirt was torn. She decided to expose herself completely to us. It was definitely a strange situation; she refused to cover herself up.

Routine Calls?

A lady called the department because an animal was in her house. When I arrived, I saw that the "animal" was a mouse. She wanted me to shoot it. I explained to her that the bullet would cause too much damage to the floor. I went over, picked the mouse up by the tail and let it loose outside.

Two old drunks got into a Domestic. Once I calmed them down, I had each of them, one at a time, put their hand on my badge, raise their right hand and promise never to argue again. It must have worked. We never received any other disturbance calls from their residence.

A woman used her key to get into her car at a local mall. She sat down in the vehicle, then realized it wasn't her car. Hers was nowhere in sight. Another woman with the same exact car called the police department and reported that she'd driven a car all the way home before she realized it wasn't hers. Same make. Same model. Same key.

Suicides seems to come in spurts. A 16 year old kid committed suicide right in front of his girlfriend, using a 30.06 rifle. His head was gone. In one year we had four suicides by hanging.

Routine Calls?

We responded to the report of a burglary. The teenage children were staying at the house when the parents were on vacation. In the bedroom, the thief had pulled open all the drawers and threw several sexually explicit photos of their parents on the floor. I'm sure the teens were embarrassed when they saw the pictures. Unfortunately for the family, we had to send the pictures to the lab for fingerprints. These very private photos were no longer private. So, if you have pictures that you don't want anyone to see, hide them where they can't be found. You never know what might happen to them, or who might see them.

When we arrived at a Domestic, the man apologized to us for snapping. He said he was tired of coming home from work every evening for the past thirty days and finding his wife had made mashed potatoes for dinner. That particular day when he came home, she wasn't around. The man then took the mashed potatoes and stuffed them in all of his wife's coat and shirt pockets. When his wife arrived home with his birthday cake and placed it on the table, he said the cake just looked like mashed potatoes to him. He picked up the cake and threw it in his wife's face. That's how the fight started.

A 911 call came in that a woman was in a bathtub having a seizure. Somehow she was able to make the call herself. When we arrived at the scene, another officer was already there. We heard muffled yells for help from him upstairs. We rushed up the stairs, ready to draw our weapons, when we stopped dead in our tracks at the bathroom door. We couldn't help but start to laugh. The officer had his hand under the woman's bottom and the other under her neck while trying to get her out of the tub. His arms slipped and his face was buried in this woman's rather well-endowed chest. The woman was fine after the seizure was over. The officer was still a little red in the face.

Routine Calls?

We arrested a man for robbing a store near the train station. He only stole enough money for the price of a train ticket. Obviously, he was desperate to get back to New York.

One afternoon I was out patrolling an area which I normally don't patrol. I was driving down the street when a woman came running towards me, screaming. Three two-year old children had fallen into a stone well in the backyard. When I got to the well, they were drowning. I ran to the garage next door, broke in and grabbed a ladder. I climbed down and grabbed onto the three children. Apparently, the three two-year olds came from the day care center next door. When the first one climbed onto the covered well, the covering collapsed, and he fell through. The other two were like church mice; they just followed the first one. I'm glad I was there to rescue these babies.

So many people abuse the 911 system. We received a call from a woman who told her children she was calling the police because they wouldn't eat their breakfast. It's people like this that make children afraid of the police.

A woman in her nineties was constantly reporting someone was in her basement. She'd call two–three times a week. We'd just keep her company for awhile, change a light bulb, or do other small things for her while we were there. She was lonely and just wanted company.

Routine Calls?

We went to a medical emergency. There was definitely a language barrier. We couldn't understand a word the man was saying. He just kept pointing to his butt. He opened the bathrobe and his intestines were hanging down to his knees. I definitely got a little queasy with this call.

I was called to a Domestic disturbance in the 'projects'. All the housing had open porches. As I was speaking with the parties involved on the landing of the second floor apartment, the male party told me he was going to leave. I advised him against that seeing how I was blocking the stairs and the only exit would be over the railing. Down below was a wrought iron fence with spikes pointing up. Before I could stop him, he hurdled the railing, jumped 25 feet, barely missing the fence below, and sprinted down the street. I still can't believe he risked getting himself killed. We arrested him a few minutes later.

I went to a burglary in progress. On the ground next to the building was the new merchandise. A man was up on the fire escape pretending to have gas pains. He was the one actually robbing the place. He thought if he faked a stomach ache, we wouldn't think he was the criminal.

A couple were making love and the woman had a .22 under her pillow. The gun went off accidentally shot the man in the butt.

Routine Calls?

I was a patrolman in 1968 when the riots erupted over the assassination of Martin Luther King. We were working two hours on and two hours off. During my break, I got to a phone and called my wife to let her know that I was alright. Standing at the pay phone and gazing down the street, it took on the appearance of a battle scene with Molotov cocktails being thrown at the officers by the crowds. It was unbelievable.

We spent a lot of hours trying to apprehend a major drug and arms dealer. When we finally had enough evidence, we got a search warrant for his house and arrested him. While there, we retrieved numerous arsenal which included several machine guns. Amongst other incriminating evidence, a VCR tape was seized. On the tape, the suspect was videotaped in various sexual positions with a woman, as well as scenes of him doing cocaine. The audio also had him telling the woman he was a drug dealer. In trying to impress the woman in the video, he also gave details concerning his drug trafficking activities. It's great when the criminals are their own worst enemy. He made the prosecution of him a lot easier.

We responded to a call by an 80 year old woman that had fallen and couldn't get up. She was lying in the middle of the bedroom floor—naked. The woman, once we helped her up, refused to put any clothes on. She said, "Once you get to be my age, clothes don't matter anymore.

I pulled up to a car parked in a secluded spot. When the couple got out of the vehicle, they were wearing each other's underwear. The pink lace really didn't do anything for the guy.

Routine Calls?

At a Domestic, the argument started between the two because the wife wouldn't let her husband go to work. She wanted him to make love to her before he went to his job. He was running late. She was a nymphomaniac.

We received a call from the neighbors that the two people next door were on their front lawn making love in the middle of the afternoon. When we arrived, they were still at it. They felt it was their property and they could do whatever they wanted, whenever they wanted, as long as it was on their property.

Years ago, at a boarding house, we were alerted by the residents of a strange odor coming from one of the apartments. The man didn't answer the door. When we got inside, we found the man dead in the closet and hanging on a hook. Somehow he must have slipped and got his collar caught on the coat hook as he was having a heart attack. It looked really strange seeing this man dead on a hook; like a scene from a horror movie.

A woman called to report her husband had died during the night. When we found the victim in bed with the covers pulled up to his neck, at first we thought he died from natural causes. My partner decided to pull down the sheets. The man had been murdered and gutted. The wife had removed his intestines and placed them in a jar in the refrigerator.

Routine Calls?

We received a call from several concerned citizens who hadn't seen their elderly male neighbor in awhile. When we arrived at the residence, the doors were locked. We gained entry through a hatchway. In searching, we found ourselves in the bedroom. I saw what seemed to be a limb of a person under some clothes in the closet. Expecting to find the gentleman dead, we lifted off the clothes and found it wasn't a body but an inflatable doll. We later established the man's relatives had taken him on a mini vacation.

One of the most rewarding days I've ever had while on the police force was when I helped a woman deliver a baby. Within three minutes of my arriving, she had given birth. For a brief time, I was able to forget about all the negative things I see while performing my duty.

One day a number of us officers were having a picnic. About a dozen of us officers, off duty of course, were in the backyard drinking beer when a guy came up to us and asked if we had any rolling papers. Almost simultaneously, we pulled out our badges. The man looked at us, turned around and left rather quickly.

The fire department put out a simple grass fire in a field. When the fire was out, we found a man had committed suicide by pouring gasoline on himself in the field and lit a flame. There was almost nothing left of the body.

Routine Calls?

We arrived at the scene of an attempted murder and suicide. The boyfriend had shot his girlfriend twice, then pulled the gun on himself. The woman, shot and bleeding, refused to let us take off her robe and look at her wounds. She was extremely modest. It took us awhile before she cooperated.

"Charlie the Chopper" decided that his manhood didn't work anymore so he didn't want it. He embedded razor blades in the window sill then proceeded to close the window. He didn't succeed completely. Some months later, a call came from a neighbor. "Charlie" was now using a hatchet. When police arrived, "Charlie" had a saw and was trying to finish the task. He still has "it" attached, but it's permanently hard now because of all the scar tissue. Whenever we see him outside with a chain saw, we get nervous.

At the scene of a Domestic, we found a smoke filled house with bacon burning on the stove. The wife had thrown bleach in her husband's face. When we arrived, she was in taking a shower in the bathroom. When asked to come out, she decided to play "Lady Godiva" without a horse. Six months later we're called back with an eviction notice. When we gained entry, still in her "Lady Godiva" suit, she punched the officer in the face.

A husband walked in on his wife and lover. The husband grabbed a knife from the kitchen and cut off his wife's lover's penis. He was more than upset about his wife's infidelity.

Routine Calls?

A man unloading a truck of slightly frozen manure accidentally got buried up to his neck. He was seriously injured; one of his legs needed to be amputated. It's hard to believe something that serious could happen to someone from manure.

Years ago we had problem, in the center of town, with the drunks at the old traffic circle. They'd come out of the bar across the street and start directing traffic.

I had the unfortunate task of notifying the ex-wife and daughter that the ex-husband/father was dead. Next door lived the aunt and another daughter. They came over; then a fight broke out. Here I was handling a duty I dread and I ended up in the middle of a Domestic.

We're there when the public needs us. One day, I went to a residence that had reported a snapping turtle on their front lawn. The turtle was gigantic. I used my night stick to pick it up and remove it off the lawn.

A white woman was pregnant by her boyfriend, a sailor who had since left port. She reported to the authorities that she was raped by a black man. The woman thought she could get a free abortion if she was raped.

Routine Calls?

A woman reported a bat in her house. When I arrived, she had a towel wrapped around her head. I grabbed the fire extinguisher to freeze the bat. Unfortunately, the fan was on in the room and everything blew back into my face. I was stunned and not the bat. Talk about feeling stupid. My second option worked. I used a broom to get it out the window.

On Thanksgiving we were called to a Domestic Disturbance. The husband and wife had gotten into an argument because he'd fed the turkey to the dog. The wife wanted her husband arrested for feeding the dog.

A homosexual, who loved to wear women's purple underwear, tried to hug and kiss one of the arresting officers at a Domestic. His significant other was violent and made lewd sexual advances directed towards the other officers. We hate whenever we get summoned to their Domestics.

We located a teenager who had been reported missing for three days. He had bruises and cigarette burns all over his body. He refused to tell us what happened to him. Finally, he admitted he'd been kidnapped, sexually abused, burned and beaten. The boy was so ashamed of what had happened to him, he didn't want to tell anyone. Here's someone who is definitely scarred for life because of some very sick individual. We arrested the perpetrator. He got off for reasons of temporary insanity. Six month later he hanged himself.

Routine Calls?

We have a problem with Southerners and Domestic Disturbances. It seems the Southerners think of their women as their property, and beating them is just teaching them a lesson. Different cultures are sometimes difficult to deal with.

In every town, I would imagine they have someone like our "Mary." I heard yelling and screaming coming from lock-up. I went to investigate. There's "Mary," a sweet little old lady, who turned and said, "What the f— do you want?" She rambled on, swearing and saying how she'd slept with JFK. Things were fine between them until Jackie came along. Supposedly, she'd even had his illegitimate son. We decided to bring her for a psychiatric evaluation. Several hours later, the doctors told us she was perfectly sane. This is the same woman who'd several weeks prior, had thrown a rock through the Marine recruiting office window because she though the officer inside was having an affair on his wife. The Marine didn't even know "Mary." She also could be seen praying for hours on someone's front lawn if they had a statue of the Virgin Mary.

We had a call one evening of a missing officer. Out on patrol, the officer had seen an open door at a garage business. He investigated. Upon entering the building, he fell into a grease pit and couldn't get out. Unable to raise him on the radio, we went in search of him. When we found him, he was rather upset, as well as slimy. But not as upset as the other officer who'd lent him his brand new jacket.

Routine Calls?

A local merchant called us one day because he found an invitation for a wedding in his dumpster. He wanted us to arrest the people for putting trash in his dumpster.

We were called to a Domestic. The husband was arrested for beating his wife. As we were leading him out in cuffs, the wife came up behind my partner and whacked the officer over the head with a frying pan. I used my cuffs on her. I hate Domestics.

A citizen called to inform us a skunk had committed suicide sometime during the night by drowning himself in their pool. We referred her to the appropriate authorities to have the skunk checked for rabies.

We have a 55 year old drunk woman in town that frequently calls the department with various complaints. Inevitably, when we arrive, she's either standing in a sheer nightgown or stuck in her bath tub. The woman has a thing for officers.

Routine Calls?

We frequently get called to the home of one of our local residents. He believes the neighbors are speaking to him through the TV set and radiators. The guy also has his telephones checked several times a year because he thinks they're 'tapped'. The man has a good job as an executive with a company and there's nothing else out of the ordinary with him, except every once in a while he'd just flip out.

A few years ago we were called to the parking lot of a known lesbian bar where a man was reported breaking into cars. When we arrived, the man was pleading with us to arrest him. Several of the women had beaten the sugar out of the vandal and he was very happy we had arrived when we did.

People sometimes abuse the 911 system. We actually got a call from a woman saying someone had stolen a pair of her underwear a few days ago. Ridiculous.

We arrived at the scene of a murder. The woman suffered from Battered Wife Syndrome and had taken a shotgun, put it in her husband's mouth and shot him a total of twelve times. She said she wanted to make sure he was dead.

A guy was up on the bridge on the other side of the railing, threatening to jump. After speaking to him for awhile, I was able to get him to shake my hand. When he did, I handcuffed him to the rail. He then decided he didn't want to jump.

Routine Calls?

We arrived at a Domestic where the wife had stabbed the husband in the stomach. We found him standing in the bathroom with his intestines in the sink. The man lived.

We obtained a search warrant for a suspected drug dealer's house. While the person and several other people in the apartment were detained in the living room on the couch, they had very cocky attitudes. One of the officers called me into the bedroom. When I came out, I asked the suspect if he was the one who'd removed the tag from the mattress. He got all upset. "No, man. It wasn't me. I bought the bed from someone else and the tag was already missing." Here we are in his apartment finding drugs and he doesn't care. I ask him about a removed mattress tag and he gets hysterical. Go figure.

A drunk had fallen asleep under an overpass. When we got close to the man, we weren't sure if he was alive or dead. We rolled him over and not only were there bugs crawling all over him, but his zipper was unzipped and his manhood was hanging out of his pants. My partner used his night stick to gently put it back into his pants before we picked him up. He was out cold.

We went to an apartment building where the neighbors had reported hearing a loud moaning and muffled screams coming from the woman's apartment. We knocked several times. There was no answer. When we entered the apartment, we found the woman on the bed, having intercourse with her German Shepherd. She was arrested for bestiality.

When we arrived at the scene of a Domestic, we knew we were at the correct address. Clothing was being tossed out the window onto the lawn.

A woman made a valiant attempt to take her own life. She went speeding down a hill, accelerating along the way. The woman then drove through bushes, hit the side of a building and eventually wound up driving through the front of a drug store. She didn't succeed in committing suicide. The car was totaled and she only had a few bumps and bruises. She said she was very disappointed that she hadn't died.

With everything I've seen over the years, from murders to accidents, there's only one time that someone actually made me sick. An elderly derelict was carrying around an old, used, filthy pillowcase. He opened up the pillow case, pulled out a greasy fish with maggots on it and started eating it in front of me. I'm getting queasy just thinking about it.

A man reported his pet snake had escaped from its cage. A small green snake. Well, I found it under the sheets of the bed and it was by no means small. It was huge. I hate snakes.

One very cold October day, a woman was running naked down a local street. She said the devil was chasing her. She refused to put on my coat until I inferred that I was Jesus Christ.

Routine Calls?

We have a local woman that purposely got her live-in boyfriend intoxicated. She took him in her car to the local bar and got him drunk. She then told him to take a taxi home and she'd follow him in a few minutes; he didn't have any money for the cab fare. She didn't follow and we had to arrest him for stiffing the cab driver. He spent the night in jail and she spent the night with another guy.

I pulled up to a parked vehicle and noticed a woman's head bobbing up and down. She was using her mouth to sexually relieve her male partner lying on the seat.

A man told his ten year old son that they were playing a game. The father put the shotgun in his own mouth and told his son to pull the trigger. The man had his own son kill him. It was terrible. This poor child has to live with the nightmare for the rest of his life.

Sometimes we encounter a few looneytoons. They aren't harmful to themselves or others; they just do crazy or odd things. We had this one guy in town spray lime not only on his lawn, but all over the outside of his house and on the driveway. Everything was white. The windows. The mailbox. The bushes. It looked like old man winter had paid a visit. Strange.

People call 911 for the most ridiculous things. A lady called to complain that when the neighbors flushed the toilet upstairs, it was too loud. She wanted them arrested for loud flushing.

Routine Calls?

We stopped a guy for speeding. His wife was in the back seat having sex with his best friend as the husband drove the car. The wife apparently was the friend's birthday present.

We received a call from the boyfriend of a married woman, wanting us to arrest the husband because he'd come home early from work, without calling or announcing himself. The husband had interrupted the wife and lover on several different occasions!

A woman decided to commit suicide. She brought a propane tank to a hotel and inadvertently blew up not only herself but the hotel room as well.

I proceeded to a house to notify the family their teenage son had just been killed in a car accident. The father answered the door. Little did I realize he was the ex-husband and there at the house to pick up his teenage daughter for the day. The ex-wife and him got into a fight. I wound up in the middle of a Domestic.

One day while I was standing directing traffic, a man came walking up to me and said he'd just stabbed his sister to death at the motel room. I thought he was kidding; he wasn't. He's now committed to an institute for the criminally insane.

Routine Calls?

My third day on the job I had a suicide. A drunk teenager had laid down on the railroad tracks and the train completely severed his head from his body. The medical examiner picked up his head and asked me if I knew him. I didn't.

A family found a boa constrictor in their basement. It had been down there for awhile, surviving on the dog's food. They noticed it when their dog started barking at his food dish from the top of the stairs.

I stopped a woman for DUI and placed her in the front of the cruiser while I informed my fellow officer of my arrest. All of the sudden, I heard over the loud speaker the woman swearing up a storm. I no longer place people in the front of my cruiser once I arrest them.

We were able to apprehend a bank robber quite easily. He'd left behind his business card in the briefcase which he'd left in the abandoned getaway car.

One night while on patrol, my partner and I were driving near the golf course when we spotted something moving on the eighteenth hole. We stopped the cruiser and proceeded to walk towards what we believed to be a person lying on the ground. What we found, much to our surprise, was not one, but two people, naked making love. They were both men.

Routine Calls?

I'm the one usually called to bizarre accidents. This time I was the victim. I was standing directing traffic when the traffic light fell on me. The pole had snapped and hit me in the chest, just missing my head. I ended up out of work for a few months.

We have a real problem in our community with satanic cults. They drop the carcasses of the animals they've sacrificed along the streets. There's always an increase of sexual assaults whenever they have their rituals. They're very difficult to apprehend.

We received several calls from neighbors that a Domestic was in progress. No one answered the door. Fearing for their safety, we took the front door down. We found the couple naked in the bathtub, making up.

The neighbors were complaining about the loud music. We knocked, no one answered. The music was almost deafening. The door was unlocked. What we saw when we entered were clothes thrown everywhere and the woman on the balcony butt naked. The man was in high heels, garters and a see-through negligee. We asked them to please turn down the music.

We received a report of a naked man, running through the neighborhood. We caught up with him breaking into a house. The man had put on the resident's bra and underwear, plus makeup.

Routine Calls?

We arrived at one hell of a Domestic/Murder/Suicide. The son stabbed his father fifteen times and his mother four times. The cross on the wall was upside down. The father was standing with the knife stuck between his ribs. The son committed suicide. When we arrived, he was unconscious—he later died. The reason he'd given his parents on why he was stabbing them was "the devil said his parents would become cabbage patch dolls if he didn't kill them."

One night while on patrol, we noticed a group of fifteen to twenty individuals, standing and gazing upwards to the sky. We stopped the cruiser and got out. Up in the sky was an enormous object, glowing and just hovering over the golf course. There was no noise coming from the craft. All of the sudden, it took off in a flash. This was our first encounter with a UFO.

We found a man dead, hanging from a tree, out in the woods, dressed in women's clothing. Some sick individuals go into the woods, tie a rope around their own necks, jump off a chair and masturbate. Then, just before they loose consciousness, use a knife to cut the rope. Unfortunately, this man passed out first.

It is possible to hang yourself from a door knob. We went to a suicide where the man tied a rope around his neck and the door knob, then laid down on the floor. He used a very short rope.

Routine Calls?

A case of housework gone bad. A lady reached into her washing machine to release her laundry load and her arm got caught in the agitator. By the time she was able to turn off the machine, her arm had become almost completely severed off. Fortunately, her arm was able to be reattached and the woman recovered. A sure case that housework can be hazardous to your health.

A woman phoned us. She was worried her son was going to hurt himself. She said he was in one of the parked cars. I came across a vehicle that looked like the pizza man's sauce had exploded. When I opened the door, I could see he more than hurt himself. His body was in the front seat and his head was in the back. I hate suicides.

One night, I saw a van parked in a secluded spot. I got out of my cruiser and knocked on the window. I could hear commotion in the back, but no one could be seen. I knocked again. Finally, I opened the door, identified myself as a police officer and asked the people to please get dressed and step outside the van. The two people, a rather large woman in her thirties and an eighteen year old man, who couldn't weigh more than 120 pounds, stepped out. The young man kept thanking me over and over again for showing up. Apparently, the obese woman was having sex with him while she had him pinned on the floor with his head wedged under the seat for almost an hour. He couldn't move. The poor kid had an indentation across his forehead from the bar under the seat.

Although Domestic Violence isn't ordinarily a funny type of call, we were summoned by a man one night to his house to settle a Domestic problem. Upon our arrival, we found the man had locked himself

Routine Calls?

in the bathroom. It took awhile before we were able to convince him that we were the police. The man's wife was not in a very humorous mood, to say the least. After finally convincing him that it was safe to come out, he told us his wife was demanding her conjugal rights. That led to an argument. He didn't want to have sex. He called the police and fled to the bathroom, locking himself in. This turned out to be a role reversal of other Domestic cases and underscores the fact that the world is changing.

A few years back, we received a call from the woman's husband. She had called her husband at work and told him she had seen what appeared to be a rather large wolf walking on its two hind legs go past her window. On the way to the house, we joked about who brought their silver bullets. When we arrived at the home, we found the woman was not a loony but a rather intelligent woman. She indicated to us the window from where she had seen the wolf. In order for her to have seen the wolf through that particular window, it would have to have been at least 9 feet tall. We went outside with our flashlights and saw under the window and around the area what appeared to be very large wolf or dog prints of just the hind feet. Now, we figured someone was playing a joke on this poor woman. We followed the tracks through the woods until we came across the neighbor's house. The two neighbors did not know each other. As we came out of the woods, he called to us and asked if we were there about the wolf. He had been sitting watching television, when he caught sight of, out of the corner of his eye, a wolf about 9 or 10 feet tall, walking on its hind feet. He said he thought he was seeing things until a few minutes later he heard a lot of commotion in the backyard. We followed him. There was a rabbit cage. On the ground around the cage we could see the wolf prints. The top of the cage had been ripped or chewed off and the two rabbits inside the cage were torn to shreds. I'm over 6 feet tall and I couldn't reach the top of the cage with my hands. We didn't find the wolf, but it's a good thing, because neither my partner nor myself had any silver bullets.

OFF DUTY REACTIONS

The question I asked the officers to respond to was, "When off duty, how do people react when they find out that you're an officer?" The responses seemed almost universal: it is a friend or acquaintance which informs others they're police officers. Instead of introducing them by just their names, it seems that the phrase, "He or she is an officer," usually gets tacked on.

It seems strange to me that the general public has a need to identify the officers by their occupation. You seldom hear people say, "This is my friend, Bob, he's a cashier at the grocery store." Or "This is Mary, she's a credit manager." "Let me introduce you to Harry, he's unemployed." So, why do we have this obsession with introducing police officers, in social settings, as being in law enforcement? This is something we've all pretty much been guilty of at one time or another.

Maybe after reading the responses from the officers, you'll give him or her a break. Don't start asking them questions about their job unless you don't mind talking about your daily duties at your own job. It's like, "Oh, so you're a mortician. How many bodies did you embalm this week?" Look beyond the profession. Treat the officers like you would anybody else.

I'm very cautious – careful. People have a tendency when introducing me to others, as always having to mention that I'm an officer. Whether it's done subconsciously to warn others or to give themselves more self–importance because they're a friend of a cop, I don't know. In a social setting, the subject of traffic tickets always comes up. Not just speeding, but running stop signs, too. It bothers me. I'd like to enjoy my life outside the uniform.

People highlight the fact, during introductions, that I'm an officer. They ask me how to go about getting a ticket fixed. Sometimes, the people go as far as asking when we're going to make our next drug bust! Others just tend to shy away from me.

Off Duty Reactions

Some people are very hateful towards officers. Others just clam up. Still others want free advice. Speeding tickets seem to preoccupy most people. Please, get a life.

While off duty, people always bring up speeding. Little do they realize that arresting someone for speeding is such a small issue in relation to the duties of an officer.

Family members and friends are the culprits. They start asking questions, mostly about speeding. Usually, when introduced to strangers, they emphasize the fact that I'm an officer. Once the people find out that I'm an officer, they usually change the subject.

I don't get the normal questions and reactions from the people that other officers get. Most have a difficult time believing I'm an officer. Once I'm out of uniform, I'm just a woman.

As a woman, they don't believe I'm an officer. To me, it's definitely a plus. I don't get bothered by questions concerning speeding tickets when I'm off duty.

I try hard to hide the fact that I'm an officer. When they do find out, people start talking about their problems. I don't like it.

Off Duty Reactions

Officers aren't exactly held in the highest esteem. They think that you're uneducated. They make jokes that you'd better behave. Then come the questions.

When I'm at a party, the temperature drops about 30 degrees once they find out I'm an officer. But the people still have to relate their ticket stories to me. They think that's all we do all day long, is write tickets. The public definitely needs to be more educated about what our real function as police officers are.

"Oh, so you're a f—ing cop." is a familiar statement. It kind of gives you that warm fuzzy feeling inside.

People get nervous around me when they find out I'm an officer. They act differently, especially in locations with alcohol. Sometimes a few people actually treat you better. But that's rare.

I don't let people know I'm an officer. Otherwise, I become the center of attention at parties and picnics. Nobody bothers me while off duty. I lead a very private life when I'm off the clock.

I don't tell them. A job is Monday through Friday, a profession is something from the inside. Off duty, I'm still a cop, 24 hours a day. It's an obligation. Yet, it should be my prerogative if I want to let people know what I do for a living.

Off Duty Reactions

Everybody wants to tell me their stores. There aren't many negative reactions to my being an officer. In fact, I find them mostly positive.

People either like you or hate you. They also can't believe that I'm an officer, so that helps.

I don't tell people. In fact, at a party one time I was asked what I did for a living. I said I worked for the town. Most people just figured I work at the town hall or something. The hostess wanted to know exactly what I did for the town. I told her that I picked up "trash," my husband almost fell off his chair. (He's also a police officer in another town.)

I work undercover, so most people don't know that I'm an officer.

Most people will change the subject once they find out that I'm an officer. Others will just stop talking to you and just walk away.

I don't tell them. Only my next door neighbor knows. It helps that I don't live in the same town I work in.

Surprised. I don't fit the stereotype of an officer. I'm by nature, kind and gentle.

Off Duty Reactions

They always have to talk about their speeding tickets or tickets for running stop signs. It never ceases to amaze me.

Some responses are good and others are bad. It's a mixture.

"You're a cop?" They can't believe it. The women like it though.

I'm always identified as a police officer when introduced by friends. People should accept me for who I am as an individual, not what I do for a living.

Questions – job related experiences. Kids always ask me whether or not I've shot anybody. Adults get nervous. I try not to tell people that I'm a cop.

Most people have a story to tell about some traffic ticket they received or they think that every cop in America knows every other cop. They tell you about some second cousin who is a cop from three states away and asks if you know them.

Off Duty Reactions

MOST BOTHERSOME CRIMINAL ACT

The question which the officers responded to for this chapter was: "What criminal act bothers you the most?" The answers I received weren't surprising at all. In fact, most of the officers added more emotion to this question than any other. By far, the most frequent responses were crimes against children – any crime. There were also a few other criminal acts that proved particularly bothersome.

Many of the officers relayed their experiences of dealing with children that had been abused. I decided *not* to relate their graphic stories to you in this book. It was extremely upsetting to me just to hear the criminal acts done to infants as young as a few months old to little preschoolers and preteens. I never realized how many people hurt, maim, torture, disfigure, sexually abuse, emotionally terrorize, and just plain physically abuse their children and others. It's appalling.

Most of the people that abuse children treat their animals with more respect. The ones which instill harm to innocent children are less than animals themselves. As one officer put it, "They're less than animals. At least animals protect their young."

You'd be very surprised to find out how many reported cases of child abuse are actually within your own city or town. What is even more shocking than the actual number of reported child abuse cases is the fact that most of these crimes aren't ever reported to the police. This is where you, as a neighbor, friend or relative should get involved. We cannot just turn our backs to crimes against kids. Could you live with yourself if you suspected a child was being abused, you didn't report your suspicions, and the child wound up scarred for life? Or worse yet, dead?

Investigating the crimes after the child has been physically and/or sexually abused is where the police officer steps in. They see the bruises and broken bones. I can see how this would have an affect on an officer – or most people for that matter. I know for a fact that the police officers I've spoken with carry these disturbing images with them, especially when they have small children of their own.

So, if you suspect that a child you know is being abused, contact your local police department and they'll instruct you on what you should do. Get involved. Save a life. Save a child.

Most Bothersome Criminal Act

Crimes against children. It's like a crime against an angel. They haven't learned about the bad stuff, yet.

Crimes against children are the worst.

Sexual and physical abuse of children.

Sexual abuse of children!

Drugs. They are the root of all evil. So many crimes are committed just so the drug addicts can support their habits. The poor children suffer because of their parents being addicts. The children aren't properly clothed or fed. They have few toys to play with because the family's money either goes up their noses or into their arms. It's a shame. So many lives are ruined because of drugs.

Acts of violence or threatened violence against a complete stranger. Primarily robbery – unprovoked by the victim.

Sexual assaults – especially repeat offenders. Even if they've served their time – it's still not enough punishment for the crime they committed. The victims have a life sentence dealing with the ordeal. Second would be selling drugs. Just seeing how drugs ruins lives is upsetting. Third is burglary.

Most Bothersome Criminal Act

Domestic violence and family members molesting children.

Child sexual abuse. It's not investigated properly. The case usually goes to a less qualified officer. People walk away most of the time. Parents don't protect their kids, i.e., a mother stands by and lets her daughter get raped by the husband – she doesn't want to divorce him or she'll lose his income. It's sick and appalling.

Child abuse and sexual assault. Both crimes should get the death penalty.

Child abuse. There's no reason for it.

Child abuse. It's heartbreaking.

Crimes against children. Neglect and child abuse. Adults can defend themselves; little children can't.

Anything to do with children. Child abuse. From not putting a child in a car seat when riding in a vehicle to beating a child for taking the last piece of their own birthday cake.

Most Bothersome Criminal Act

Rape. Sexual assault. Especially when it happens to little kids.

Child molestation.

Drunk drivers.

Crimes against women and children – they should be castrated. We should have electric bleachers instead of chairs. I definitely believe capital punishment is a viable solution.

Child crimes.

Anything to do with children.

Crimes against children.

Juvenile sexual assaults.

Anything to do with children.

Most Bothersome Criminal Act

■— Crimes against children.

■— Child Abuse.

■— Violence with children.

■— Crimes against children.

■— Child molestation and rapes. I'd be willing to castrate them myself.

■— Rapists, child molesters and crimes against the elderly.

■— Sex offenses – especially with children.

■— Crimes against poor innocent children.

■— Sexual assault against children. We had seven complaints filed last week alone, and we're a smaller community.

Most Bothersome Criminal Act

Crimes against children. The criminals should be castrated first, then they should be put to death.

The physical and sexual abuse of children who are so little and helpless to defend themselves.

CREATE YOUR OWN LAW

When I interviewed the officers for this chapter, they were asked, "If you could create a law that would be enforced, what would it be and why?" The first thing a majority of the officers said was, "No plea bargaining!" The actual responses to the officers being given their own law to create varied, depending upon their function and duties within the Department. Undercover narcotics officers' responses were different from the regular patrolman's answers, just as the Chiefs' responses differed from the detectives' opinions of what law he or she would create.

This is a very important question. These answers are from the public servants who encounter criminals and law breakers on a daily basis. They, perhaps better than our own legislature, know where the problems are within our state. Taking the question one step further, while interviewing the hundreds of officers, another opinion surfaced. We need the laws, but our prisons and legal system are viewed as "a joke."

The majority of the law enforcement here in Connecticut believe the criminals run the jails, don't serve anywhere near the time to which they have been sentenced and the prisoners have more rights and privileges than the regular law abiding citizens. There are more drugs in the prisons than people would like to believe. The criminals come out in better shape because of their workout rooms. They can mingle with other prisoners and learn better ways to steal or deal drugs.

Our jails aren't prisons, they're more like country and social clubs. They've got their cable TV, hot meals, in some, better law libraries than most of our Municipal and State Police Departments, and we the people of the State of Connecticut are paying for all of it. Whatever happened to jail being a punishment? These people broke the law and don't have to worry about working or how they're going to put food on the table for the children like we do. In some prisons, we even pay them unemployment.

The general consensus was that we can create as many laws as we wish but they need to be enforced and the sentences need to be served. We need stiffer penalties and prisons, not resorts. The prisoners shouldn't have more rights than their victims. They should, as a consequence of their crimes, be stripped of all their rights.

As one officer put it, "Once you commit a crime, you have all the rights in the world. We, as regular law-abiding citizens, have no rights." How true!

Here are a few of the responses I received . . .

Create Your Own Law

Mandatory death sentence for dealing narcotics. Take out the profit in dealing drugs, then most of the crimes wouldn't be committed.

Domestic law concerning the violation of a restraining order where the victim has invited the person back to their house. Then, when things get dicey, we're called. Even if the one with the restraining order tells us they were invited, we are obligated to arrest them. The person which encouraged the violation of the restraining order should be arrested for "conspiracy to violate a restraining order." This is such a problem. We want to help but repeat offenders have been much too common for too long.

Domestic Restraining Order; conspiracy to violate the restraining order.

Stupidity. It should be against the law to be a moron.

There are already too many laws, some of which aren't enforceable.

I believe in capital punishment – a life for a life. Also, juveniles should be treated as adults – even as young as 12 years old. Especially, for the more serious crimes. Too many gangs have influence over these juveniles and peer pressure adds to their committing of serious crimes. They know they'll only get a slap on the wrist.

Create Your Own Law

_____ Being just plain stupid. Not using common sense.

_____ Protective orders – inviting them in, then something goes wrong – both should be arrested.

_____ Mandatory: 20 years without parole for sexual molestation of children.

_____ There should be no plea bargaining. Community service should be to clean up the streets, e.g., garbage, for any crime that wasn't violent.

_____ No plea bargaining for crimes against children. We need to enforce the laws that are already on the books. All violent crimes shouldn't have plea bargaining either.

_____ Spitting. It's disgusting.

_____ Stricter penalties on juvenile crimes.

_____ Stealing cars should have stiffer penalties.

Create Your Own Law

The death penalty should be enforced and publicly aired on television. Connecticut is just too liberal.

12 years and older should be tried as adults.

Community service for adults not putting their children in car seats.

Sexual assault: castration. No plea bargaining!

Should have the Singapore law enforcement system. Mandatory sentence is a joke because they get out on good behavior.

Domestic violence – three strikes and you get to go to jail for awhile.

Child molesters are only treated as a social problem. Tougher penalties should be imposed.

DUI's which take the life of another only serve a few years. Send them to Siberia for their sentence. Connecticut prisons are a joke.

Crimes committed while using a handgun should receive mandatory sentences, without plea bargaining or being paroled early.

Create Your Own Law

No plea bargaining if a weapon or gun is used in the commission of a crime.

Treat as adults, anyone 12 years old and up, for violent and drug related crimes.

Domestic violence: conspiracy to violate a protective or restraining order.

Being an asshole without a permit.

If you ask a girl out for a date, she can't say, "No."

Child abuse and molestation should follow you in the computer. Pedophiles can't be rehabilitated.

Stupidity: having a terminal case of their head up their ass.

Old people can't drive. Mandatory retesting every year after age 62.

Create Your Own Law

Giving an officer the middle finger should be considered a criminal act.

No plea bargaining. There should be a mandatory death penalty for violent crimes and drug related crimes. Castration is the only way to go for rapists and child molesters.

Narcotics: life sentence with no plea bargaining and no parole.

Domestic violence: stiffer sentences. There should be mandatory imprisonment of 30 days for the first offense.

Heavier penalties for dealing and the use of drugs. They have to stop just giving them a slap on the wrist.

Being an asshole without a permit – having their heads stuffed up their asses should be a crime.

No plea bargaining whatsoever. Also, in regards to domestic violence – conspiracy to violate a restraining or protective order. Too many times we're used as pawns by the so-called victims.

Create Your Own Law

Mandatory death sentence for any sexual assault against a child.

Any sale of narcotics to minors or children should have no plea bargaining and no suspended sentences. Kids are our future.

If someone commits murder, it should be, an eye for an eye.

If you use a weapon of any type in the commission of a crime, you should serve a minimum of five years without good time, sentence reduction or any incarceration privileges.

Anyone arrested and successfully prosecuted for sexual assault, especially to children, should be castrated or the equivalent.

Create Your Own Law

ACCIDENTS AND INCIDENTS

"What was the most bizarre accident you ever were called to?" is the topic of this chapter. This is one question most of the officers really didn't want to talk about. It is understandable, especially when they see so many people injured and dying, or worse yet, dead. The memories and flashbacks they have concerning a number of the accidents is all too common for many of these officers.

I've written this chapter without too much graphic detail. I'm sure you can use your imagination as to what a scene where someone has been killed would probably look like. If you want blood and guts, it would be better if you just rented a movie. The officers did, however, describe to me in detail a few of the accidents. For several officers, it was overwhelming to recount particular accidents, especially the ones where they were unable to save the lives of those severely injured.

One thing I think most people forget is the officer has to maintain control of a situation without letting his or her emotions get involved. At the scene of an accident, it is the job of the officer to get the facts, while also providing comfort to those injured until the ambulance arrives. One thing in particular that adds more aggravation to an already distressing situation are those people passing the accident who find it necessary to rubber neck. People seem to want to see the blood, guts and gore. When the passerby slows down or impedes traffic while an officer is trying to save the lives of those injured, it just makes the situation worse. When you see an accident where the officers have already made it to the scene, don't stop to take a look. You'll end up causing the traffic to back up and potentially even be the cause of additional accidents.

Be responsible; let those officers and medical emergency personnel do their jobs. Imagine if it was you or a loved one that was injured in an accident. Wouldn't you want the officers to be paying attention to your needs, instead of having to go over to a stopped motorist and tell them to get moving? Too many times, accidents are life and death situations.

Also, remember that driving a car is a privilege which carries a lot of responsibility. Your life and the lives of your passengers, as well as other motorists, are the responsibility of the driver. Pay attention. Obey the laws. Slow down for construction workers. But most importantly of all, don't drink and drive.

Accidents and Incidents

One day while off duty, I witnessed the most incredible accident. A motorcyclist coming the opposite direction, crossed the center line and hit the T-top car in front of me, head on. On impact, the man slid up the hood of the vehicle. By the time I got to the car, the driver was standing outside the T-top. I asked him where the motorcyclist was. He just pointed inside the car. Sprawled in the passenger seat was the guy. Fortunately, he only suffered a broken leg.

A man driving a Camaro had hit a telephone pole sideways and split the car in half. The driver of the vehicle was still sound asleep in the front half of the car when I arrived. He wasn't even injured.

The linkage broke on a woman's car. She went speeding past the police station; we could hear her screaming. She had burnt her brakes out and couldn't stop. The woman proceeded across the high school field and wound up on the top of a giant flower pot. She wasn't injured. The woman said she didn't even think of turning the car off.

A man was hit by a dump truck and ejected from his car. The man's life was saved because he landed in a pile of manure. He'd lost his glasses in the manure. I had to retrieve them for him.

A motorcyclist was driving down the road one night and hit a deer. The bike and deer were okay until the startled animal got up. It ran towards the guy and punctured him with his antlers. The deer was a little peeved about being hit.

Accidents and Incidents

Back in the sixties, I was sitting on the side of the highway over an underpass. I could see in my rearview mirror, two convertibles doing at least 90 mph. They decided to go down the ramp just before me. The second car caught the guard rail and spun like a top on its front bumper, then landed directly on the top of the other car. Parts from the vehicles flew everywhere. They both came to a rest under the overpass I was sitting on in my cruiser. When I got down to the cars, I had expected to find at least two dead people. Much to my surprise, I saw the car on top being pushed over. Both the people were fine; only a few bumps and bruises. It took two tow trucks and two dump trucks to pick up all the pieces of the cars.

A woman left her small children in the car with the engine running. The car was somehow thrown into reverse. The vehicle ended up hitting numerous parked cars. The children were seriously injured and had to be taken to the hospital by Life Star helicopter.

A woman driving a Camaro at around 80 mph hit a bump in the road, became airborne and landed on the top of a van going in the opposite direction. She was DOA.

A car driven by a seventeen year old and his sixteen year old girlfriend ended up driving off a high bank in a back parking lot. The car got stuck standing on end. They weren't injured. The couple saw a hotel next door and had decided, instead of parking in the car, they'd drive over to the hotel. There was no access, only a steep drop.

Accidents and Incidents

One very icy winter day, I was called to the first of many accidents. The roads were glare ice. At the scene of the one car accident, I found the victim – dead and slumped over the wheel. All of a sudden, there's another accident. Before I could reach the second vehicle, two more cars smashed up. It was terrible. I wasn't sure which accident or victims to run to first. Don't drive in icy weather if you don't have to. It's not worth risking your life over, or for that matter, giving a police officer the makings of a nervous breakdown.

At two in the morning, I received a call that a tractor trailer truck had driven off the bridge. I thought it was a joke; it wasn't. Down in the river below, I could see the truck upside down in the water. When I rescued the man from the river below, he only had a broken leg. He told me as we were putting him into the ambulance, I've never had a thrill like that before and I hope I never do again.

I stopped a car one evening because they didn't have their headlights on. When I approached the vehicle, the headlights came on. As I got back to my cruiser, the car started to drive off. All of a sudden, the lights went off again just as the car took a left turn. A motorcyclist coming the other direction was hit by the car. I rushed over. The femur of the motorcyclist was sticking out his back pants pocket. He was pretty banged up. Apparently, the car had a short in the electrical system. Fortunately, the injured man is able to walk again.

I dread Prom nights. I was traveling down the road one evening, when a bunch of cars began pulling over and stopping. I knew there had been an accident. Two brothers, which I knew personally, had.just been killed in a car crash. I can still see the images in my mind.

Accidents and Incidents

At the scene of a DUI accident, I was escorting the intoxicated woman back to the cruiser. She was in high heels, a mini skirt and a skimpy top with no bra. Just as we got to my car, she stumbled and I tried to catch her before she fell. Unfortunately, when I did, my right hand slipped up her short skirt and my left hand missed her shoulder as I caught her left breast. Just then, my sergeant pulled up to ask me if I needed assistance. Talk about an embarrassing situation. At least she didn't fall and hurt herself.

The D.O.T. was doing construction work on the bridge. They had placed the jersey barriers up so that no one could drive where there was no longer tar but only steel beams. Well, this Oriental man who didn't speak a word of English, drove around the barriers and got stuck on the bridge deck, with all four tires hanging in mid-air.

A vehicle was speeding as it went over a hill. While airborne, it hit the guide wires. The driver was ejected from the vehicle and hit a telephone pole with his face. The passenger was also killed when the car landed upside down.

A woman was traveling in an excess of 100 mph and rolled the car over half a dozen times. She landed upside down, still strapped in her seat belt. She asked what had happened; she wasn't injured at all.

Accidents and Incidents

I was called to a diner for a disturbance. Another cruiser, rushing to an emergency, hit another vehicle. I ran to help. It was dark. I could hear moaning coming from the bushes; it was the driver of the car. She'd been ejected from her vehicle upon impact. The woman died in my arms.

For as long as I live, I will never forget that July 31st. It's not only my wedding anniversary, but also the day I arrived at a horrible accident. A woman, whose car had been hit from behind, was lying in the middle of the street. She wasn't wearing any pants. As I was administering CPR, I kept wondering to myself, "Where are her pants?". Another officer came over to me and told me to stop; she was gone. The woman had been severed from the neck to her waist and I couldn't save her. The girl had been hit so hard by the impact of the other vehicle, she was literally ripped out of her pants as she was ejected out the back window of the car. Her girlfriend was lying on the hood of the vehicle. At first, I didn't see the other car. It had been pushed down the embankment. There were a total of four victims and one had died. Apparently a guy traveling at an excessive rate of speed tried passing her on the right side of the vehicle, lost control and slammed into her car. The dead girl's father could be seen, everyday, sitting on the side of the road, next to where his daughter had been killed. It's been fourteen years, and I still can't forget that accident. I have to pass that way everyday I go to work.

There was a four car accident as a result of a deer crossing the road. The deer ran into the first vehicle, then bounced off, landing on a car going in the opposite direction. The second car then hit a third car and the third hit a fourth vehicle. All this damage because a deer wanted to get to the other side of the street.

Accidents and Incidents

I was only a few hundred feet down the ramp when the motorcyclist was hit by a van in the westbound lane and thrown over the barriers into the eastbound lane of the highway. The man landed right in the path of a woman who was nine months pregnant and he was dragged a distance under her car before she could stop. The van decided to get off the exit without putting his blinker on or checking the lane and slammed right into the motorcyclist. The victim didn't have many cuts on his body. He was killed instantly, though. When I looked around, I saw the dead man lying there, the pregnant woman screaming hysterically and pieces of the motorcycle were everywhere. Suddenly, I felt so helpless. Fortunately, the guy in the van had come around to the eastbound lane, parked his van on the side of the road and just stood there, staring at the accident. A few witnesses identified the driver and we were able to apprehend him. This was such a senseless accident.

As I approached the scene of an accident, the woman with five kids in the car – not wearing seat belts – immediately drove off. She proceeded down the road and smashed into a tree, tossing the children around like ping pong balls. Senseless.

We had a report of an accident. When we arrived to investigate, at first we didn't see any vehicle. The car had hit a bump, became airborne, missed the trees and landed in someone's fenced backyard

The driver had rolled the car eight or nine times and was ejected from the vehicle. The man was quite large. When he was thrown from the car, his head hit a tree. The man was dead before we arrived. We didn't move the body until the medical examiner arrived.

Accidents and Incidents

When we rolled him over, underneath was a slender woman, dead. She had also been ejected and hit the tree head on as well.

One day while on patrol, one of the other officers decided to check out a local factory which used to be a military facility – complete with missile silos. The road was curvy. Somehow, the officer left the road and landed directly on the top of an old missile silo. It took three officers and a wench to remove the cruiser.

A young woman hit a buck deer with her car. The car was completely demolished. I told her I had to shoot the deer because it had two broken legs and possibly internal bleeding. She ran to the deer's side, grabbed it around the neck and hugged it. That's when the deer bucked her and broke her nose. The deer was about 150 pounds and still strong enough even though it was dying. The girl didn't want me to kill the deer and kept blocking my aim. I didn't know whether to shoot the deer or her.

There was glare ice on the highways as I arrived at the scene of an accident. I set up flares and witnessed another five accidents all within one minute. I called on my radio. There goes another one, and another one. Please send help. Oh, no. There's another one . . .

Four young boys, two of which were brothers, were sitting on the guardrails, waiting for their mothers to come and pick them up after their baseball game. One of the friends had just gotten up to walk around, when a drunk driver smashed right into the two brothers

Accidents and Incidents

and friend, killing them instantly. The scene was horrible; parts of their small bodies were everywhere. The fourth child was badly injured. The drunk had no remorse. He said, "Now there's four less bastards in the world." He had deliberately run into the children.

We were in pursuit of a stolen vehicle. The chase went on for miles. The auxiliary officer riding with me had a 357 with a six inch barrel. I pulled alongside the suspect and he tapped the window with his gun. The suspect finally decided to stop but lost control and slammed into a telephone pole.

Late one evening, I was called to a one car accident. When I reached the driver's window, I whacked my head on the door frame of the vehicle. The woman was fine except she had been driving around without any clothes on.

I arrived at the scene of a terrible accident. Two cars were on fire and the two children ages one and three were severely injured because neither were in car seats. Another adult was trapped in the car plus another person was injured and lying in the middle of the street. It seemed like there were bodies everywhere and people were crying.

There had been a report of a truck accident. The officer arrived and saw smashed vehicles everywhere. He couldn't believe his eyes. This had to be, by far, the worst accident scene he'd ever been to. Come to find out, it was only a one vehicle accident. The truck had been carrying the other squashed vehicles to the scrap yard when the accident occurred.

Accidents and Incidents

I was summoned to an accident and told over the radio there were no injuries. When I arrived at the scene, the four people involved in the crash were dead.

My partner and I were called to an accident involving an ambulance. When we arrived, a man was lying on a stretcher in the ambulance – dead. We thought at first he had died as a result of the accident. We later found out he was a patient being rushed to the hospital for a heart attack. It was strange.

An unmanned Monte Carlo being warmed up in the winter time, slipped into reverse and kept smashing cars as it made a larger and larger circle.

A very distinguished gentleman and his attractive female passenger were involved in an accident. The car sustained about a thousand dollars worth of damage. He didn't want the accident reported. I don't think it was his wife in the car with him.

A young male motorist who had been stopped on numerous occasions for speeding violations was the victim of a bizarre accident. He'd just left a party – drunk – and decided to smash mailboxes with his vehicle. While plowing over the mailboxes, ironically, he hit a speed limit sign. It kicked up, flew through the passenger window of the car and plunged itself through the driver's head like an arrow. As serious as his injury was, when I arrived, with the sign post protrud-

Accidents and Incidents

ing from both sides of his head, he was attempting to leave the scene of the accident. He was oblivious to his injury. Fortunately, the auto was stuck on a mound of dirt. The victim survived and so did the missing passenger we found out about a short time later. The passenger had been so stunned by the accident and his friend's condition, that he had fled into the woods. About 30 minutes later, we received a phone call from the passenger, reporting the accident. He thought he'd be arrested for failure to report the accident.

A man was run over by a bulldozer at a local construction site. He was flattened into the ground. Would you believe he lived and suffered no permanent injuries?!

An elderly woman backed her car out of the driveway. In doing so, she hit two houses even before she made it onto the street.

The most bizarre accident I ever witnessed was a cement truck that drove right off a bridge. I never saw him hit the brakes.

A bread truck hit a curb and wound up stuck on the top of guide wires. It was just hanging there in midair when we arrived. The driver was a little shaken, but alright.

A couple of teenagers went four-wheeling. Their jeep went over a cliff and got stuck standing straight up. Neither of the boys were injured, but it took a considerable amount of time before the jeep was back on its four wheels again.

Accidents and Incidents

A guy left a bar drunk and hit a fire hydrant. The man died at the scene. In the back seat of the car, we saw these little green objects floating in the blood on the floor. We couldn't figure out what they were at first. It looked strange. Later, we found they were cherry tomatoes with their green tops still attached.

We arrived at the scene of a head-on collision where we found the victim dead with his head up over the dashboard. As I felt for a pulse, I turned to my partner and said, "He's dead." Then all of a sudden, I hear a voice that said, "No I'm not." Under the dashboard was the man's young son.

Two young kids stole a car. They were too short to steer and work the gas at the same time. So, one juvenile worked the gas pedal while the other steered the vehicle right into four other cars. They forgot to work the brake.

At an accident, one woman had rear-ended another woman. The woman in front had stopped for traffic during the morning rush hour. The woman in the second vehicle was late for work and was still straightening her bra when the hook came undone. She attempted to hook her bra up while leaning forward on the steering wheel and reached back with her other hand. By the time she noticed the traffic in front of her had stopped, it was too late. Fortunately, no one was seriously injured.

It was "human error." A pregnant mother with her two year old in the van had a head-on collision. Witnesses said she had crossed over four lanes before striking the oncoming vehicle. CPR failed; the two year old died. The woman and her unborn child were also dead. It was around Christmas time. The toddler was buried with a teddy bear, a present from Santa. The husband said, "I just lost my entire family, my entire world, and I'll never know how or why it happened."

Accidents and Incidents

OFF THE CLOCK DIFFICULTIES

"Is it difficult to leave your job out of your personal/home life once you're off the clock?" was the question asked of the officers. The responses were often mixed by the individual officers. At first, most would say, "No." Then thirty seconds later they were relating an incident that was quite the opposite.

I have definitely formed several opinions concerning the responses I received. It appears that in the medium to large municipal police departments that officers tend to spend more time socially with fellow officers. Very few speak with their wives or girlfriends about their jobs. They have a tendency to not only drink more off duty, but to also have more difficulty in personal relationships. There's a definite reason for this; they see more crimes if only because of the size of the populations they patrol.

The smaller departments generally have more stress within the police department. Not all of them; and neither do I mean to indicate the medium and larger departments don't have stress inside their respective departments. It goes without saying, that there is some level of stress in every department. Law Enforcement officers face life threatening situations more than any other non-military job on a day-to-day basis. The officers frequently see not only the bad elements of our society, but accidents and violence as well.

It's the officers who are able to find a release, either through a spouse, friend or therapist, and are able to consciously separate their jobs from their personal lives, that are without the constant stress. Just as it's difficult for you to separate yourself from your work when there's a high level of stress; it's just as hard, if not more difficult for a police officer.

It's very difficult, if not impossible. You see the worst in people. For example, how can I go home and forget that I saw how an 11 year old kid accidentally shot and killed by a 9 year old child. It stays with you. I don't even speak to my wife about it. I lost half my friends when I became a police officer. The "choir practices" helped me get through a lot of rough times.

Off the Clock Difficulties

I have no choice but to leave it out of my personal life. I have two small children which are my responsibility to be a father to.

Sometimes it's difficult. People ask me for my help when I'm off duty. I try not to let it affect my life even though I realize that people look at me differently.

No, I go home and it's my time. On duty and off duty are separate. I don't go out drinking with the other officers after work.

I don't want to bring my job home. I don't speak to my wife about my work day.

I don't bring my personal life to my job and vice versa. I don't talk to my wife about work. In fact, when I was injured on the job, I didn't have them notify my wife until I was getting ready to go into the operating room.

Yeah, it's difficult. It gets involved with my personal life, especially since I work undercover.

It's difficult. Especially when I've been involved in so many drug busts.

Off the Clock Difficulties

The first few years I took the job a little too seriously while off duty. I always carried my weapon. Now, I'm more relaxed when I'm off duty. Of course, at times, my wife does need to remind me when I react too harshly or seem condescending while at home with her and the kids. I'm always paying attention to people when I'm off duty, though. One time while eating at a restaurant, I noticed a convicted felon we'd been trying to locate for some time, eating at another table. I called for backup and we apprehended him.

It's tough to eliminate the sight and/or smell of an accident. It's even more difficult to forget the 14 month old baby which you had just left at the hospital for being sexually abused. It's especially difficult when you have small children of your own at home.

It's not difficult. I don't take things personally. I don't worry about my job when I'm off duty. I still always carry my radio, but that's not a negative point. Unconsciously, I still look at license plates for expired stickers.

No, it's not difficult at all. I stay away from the department on my days off. I don't have a scanner at home. I'm very much involved in sports.

It's difficult sometimes, only because my husband and I are both police officers in the same department. You can't help but to talk about work.

Off the Clock Difficulties

I handle it fairly well. Although there are some cases in which I asked to be called on at any time of day or night.

Of course it's difficult. Especially during a continuing murder investigation. You just can't stop thinking about it.

No. I don't talk about my job. I don't have the desire to relive the day. I've made a career out of separating my personal life from being an officer. I lead a very private life. I do spend a lot of time acting, though.

No, of course it's not difficult. It only takes me three days of vacation to almost forget about work. It's never out of your mind totally, though.

Yes, it's difficult. You can't get away from it.

Smaller departments do a better job of screening, so it's not difficult.

Not really. It helps to be a "sick unit."

Off the Clock Difficulties

No, it's not difficult. I don't talk to my wife about my job. I don't bring my job home.

I have no problem separating the two. I work out a lot, plus running helps to relieve the stress from the job. I don't talk about work outside of work. I don't want to talk about the serious crimes, accidents and/or murders. People are always wanting advice on tickets. I am an officer 24 hours a day. You can't leave the fact that you're a police officer just because you aren't wearing a uniform.

Yes, it's difficult. I talk to my wife, especially since you see so much. It's tough when you're off duty and you take the car home with you. I always feel like I have to be doing my job, even when I'm off the clock.

Yes, sometimes. I'm involved in a lot of other emergency related things.

Yeah. You develop an attitude; you're used to having your own way. You're expected to take charge. It requires a conscious effort to separate the two.

No, not at all. I don't mix business with pleasure.

Off the Clock Difficulties

Yes. I'm only human. You're definitely influenced by your job. You carry it with you. I try not to talk to my wife about work. I do talk to my twelve year old son, though. He wants to become an officer someday.

Sometimes. It depends on how my shift went; if I had a bad night, or it was rough, funny or exciting. I'm like a pendulum – swinging from one emotion to the next.

No, I don't take my job home, except for the crimes against children because I've got children of my own.

You insulate yourself but it still bothers you.

Sometimes it's tough. My husband is a police officer in another department. We're each other's support.

It's very difficult at times. Especially since I have children. My wife is my sounding board and my support.

Off the Clock Difficulties

In the beginning it was difficult. But as time goes on, you learn to separate the two as much as possible. To bring your work home with you can only spell disaster if one is married with a family.

When you're the Law, the telephone keeps ringing. People's misfortunes and grief over the loss of loved ones cannot be left behind when you leave the office.

Off the Clock Difficulties

CRIME PREVENTION

The topic of this chapter is: "If you were given the opportunity to speak to the public concerning crime and/or prevention of crime, what would be your message?" The most commonly heard response: *Get involved!*

A lot of the police officers do have the opportunity at one time or another to speak to the public concerning prevention of crime, and their message is to get involved. The Police Departments have officers available to speak to the communities and children in our schools. They have an incredible commitment to the D.A.R.E. program and are available to help set up block watches. Every single Police Department has brochures available to the general public, usually in the foyer of the department, on topics ranging from crime prevention to what you can expect if you get stopped for DUI.

The police are there to provide a public service. Take advantage of their knowledge, community programs and pamphlets. But most of all, get involved. It's better to make a call to the police or stop by and get information on prevention of crime, than to be filing a report on the possessions that were stolen when you were at work or out of town.

Public awareness - get involved. If you see a suspicious person, call us. The public is our eyes. We appreciate the tips. You may be saving someone's life or possessions.

People need to get involved. Towns like Stonington, Glastonbury and Old Saybrook, just to name a few, have a Citizen Police Academy. This in itself has, through public relations, made our Department more service oriented.

People should be aware that 90% of crimes committed are related in one way or another to drugs.

Crime Prevention

Given the opportunity to speak to the public, my concern would be to make people more aware of DUI and it's consequences.

We're all in the same boat. The public is going to have to assist. The police are only as good as the public they serve.

Protect your own. Everyone should know how to use a weapon.

Prevention of crime - people are only concerned with themselves. If a neighbor has a problem - Get Involved!

If you see a crime, please report it. Get involved.

Be a witness; report crimes, but also stay out of harm's way. Do *not* get involved in any threatening situation. Leave the law enforcement to the police.

Report crimes, help others and get involved. Neighborhood watches alone aren't always that effective. We need to get back to the family values; teaching right from wrong, even though a lot of families are headed by single parents. Children learn by example.

Crime Prevention

Get involved. Don't be anonymous when calling in. We will protect your identity. You may have more helpful information.

Security measures - practice the use of safety devices. They may be good in theory, but you need to know how to use them. Turn the alarm on at your house. If it's not on - it won't work.

Be alert. Be aware of your surroundings. Also, don't be a part of the problem, e.g., buying stolen merchandise. If the cost of something is too good to be true, it probably is.

If a crime is committed, call the police. Report the crime. Take back your streets; we'll lose them if we're not careful. Be more concerned. Make it your city or town again. Take action!

The public has an equal responsibility. We're only as good as the information and support from the citizens. It's a partnership between the community and the police.

Get involved!

Crime Prevention

Crime is everybody's problem. People are naive. They make it easy for criminals to steal their possessions by leaving the garage door open and cars unlocked. You're inviting trouble. If you see a crime or something suspicious, call the police. It's our job to be bothered. Citizens can do more. Block watches, etc.

Be aware of your surroundings.

Since most people are concerned about crime relating to their possessions, find ways to make the access to your home more difficult. We can help you. Give us a call or stop by. That's what we're here for.

Use common sense.

I'd talk about DUI. People should buckle up and have a designated driver if they plan on drinking that night. Also, parents should get more involved.

Don't be stupid. A good example is a cemetery where a number of robberies had occurred. A woman left her car door open, her purse on the seat and her keys in the ignition. Her purse got stolen. She wanted to know what she could have done to have prevented the robbery. First, take your keys out of the ignition, put your purse under the seat and lock the door. Simple.

I would make people aware that 90% of the crimes are drug related. This also includes alcohol, because it's considered a drug as well.

Be aware and participate as concerned citizens. 93% of the people aren't affected by crime and they're the ones always making value judgments without participating in notifying us of crimes they've seen.

The message to the public needs to be that if you remain uninvolved in your community and neighborhood, by the time you realize any problems with criminal activity, it will probably be too late to reclaim your neighborhood. You'll be saying, "It used to be a nice neighborhood." People need to get involved if they want to maintain their quality of life.

Crime Prevention

PUBLIC PERCEPTION

I asked the officers, "What do you dislike the most of the public's perception of you and your job?" The overall attitude was frustration. If you recall in the introduction, I stated that one of the main reasons I decided to write this book was because of the negative perception the general public has in regards to police officers.

When you pick up a newspaper which has a story concerning an officer, it's seldom something positive. News, after all, is considered something out of the ordinary. Not normal. That's why they're called newspapers. One bad apple definitely spoils the pie, especially when the pie is made up of police. We trust them to do their jobs, and when one of them violates our trust, we should know about it and make sure that it won't happen again. Yet, we know it probably will. All we can do is try to prevent others from breaking the laws themselves.

There are corrupt people in every facet of life. In your office, there's probably someone who took an idea of yours or someone else's and promoted it to their superiors as their own. Or someone that got arrested for embezzling funds. Does that mean to say everyone in your profession or job is corrupt? When it comes to police officers, though, it's magnified.

Who do you call when there's an accident or your house gets burglarized? The police. Who do you contact when your child runs away from home or the neighbor is having a noisy party at one in the morning? The police.

Do they expect to be thanked for every good thing they do, both while on duty and off? No. Just don't crucify them or stereotype the officers as being a negative force just because the officer gave you a ticket for speeding or arrested you for DUI. He or she is just doing what we pay them to do—their job.

> People fail to recognize humans make mistakes. We, as police officers, are still, to the best of my knowledge, considered as part of the human race. We have feelings, too. You need to respect the fact that it's a job. Off duty, I'm off duty. I'm far from perfect.

Public Perception

Fortunately, the reputation of this Department is about 10–1 in favor of the police. We take pride in our Department and it shows.

They automatically think that we're crooked or dishonest. They think we personally have something to gain by giving them a ticket. The people believe that it's like, "Gee, if I write two more tickets I can win a free microwave or three more and I can win a trip to the Bahamas." It's ridiculous.

They think that you don't do anything. Especially if you're having a cup of coffee. They don't see those times where you didn't have a lunch break, or spent time working on a case—off the clock. In fact, these citizens even went so far as to try and do away with our Department.

People think that all police are bad. We have feelings. We have families. People are quick to prejudge by the actions of a few.

The public thinks that we're donut eating, coffee drinking, out of shape police officers. Incidentally, I eat twinkies, so I don't get the crumbs on my uniform.

Public Perception

We are the only profession that goes looking for trouble. The job is essentially common sense and blind luck. They complain when we're seen in coffee shops eating donuts every morning. Well, I see you there every morning, too. Don't a lot of people eat donuts and drink coffee?

The public thinks we've got it too easy and we're always in the coffee shop.

Thinking that most officers take graft or are always getting something for free—like coffee. I guess the second part about getting free or half priced meals might get other people upset. A few years back, I realized the public might take a different view of a free cup of coffee. Now, I make it a point to not accept the free coffee, etc.

People get amnesia. They forget the fact that we're there to enforce the law. They forget that we're there to help them.

The public thinks we should know the answers to everything. They'll even call the emergency number to find out the score of the rival football game which is still in progress. Landlord vs. tenant questions. You name it, they expect us to know the answer.

Public Perception

People's obsession with speeding statutes. It's such a minor part of the job. Also the stereotyping of one bad officer or incident and then all officers are labeled "bad."

Most people think that all white cops are bad. Racism. When people call us for assistance, they have attitudes as soon as we arrive. They called us. We didn't phone them. We're there to help them with their complaint and when we start asking questions, they think we're harassing them. We don't treat anyone any different from the next.

There is no respect like there was in the past for law enforcement officers. If we're not to a call immediately, they get upset and start yelling at us.

They expect us to solve all their problems. We're not psychiatric doctors, although I feel like it at times.

They automatically think we're racially prejudiced.

The community thinks the job is easy. You know, drink coffee and eat donuts all day long. We don't eat donuts anymore—we eat croissants and bagels—it's the 90's thing to do.

Public Perception

We're not heroes as they expect. The TV glorifies only 10% of the real job. I don't like it.

Yes, I'm a public servant. The public pays you and they expect you to do whatever they want you to do. Also, people think the police department itself is an adequate facility; officers are actually stumbling over each other. How would they like to have an office they have to share with five other people, when it should only hold one for such a small space?

I hate when people use us as the boogie man with small children. For instance, the mother tells the child that if they don't behave, the officer will arrest them. The parent is sending the wrong message to their child concerning the function of a police officer.

Nobody likes cops, both criminals and victims alike. People think that we have a TV mentality.

The people see the uniform and not the face or personality. We are non-people—void of individual characteristics.

The public stereotypes us as donut-eating cops. For your information, I love donuts, but I won't eat them in public. I've become a closet donut eater. They also believe that all we do is give out tickets like robots.

Public Perception

It seems that one bad officer becomes world news, yet our good deeds only get a clap, if we're lucky. Compared to the athletes and entertainers which are positive, officers save lives and our overall perception is still negative.

People watch too many cop shows. They become armchair cops. They think that all officers are like the ones seen on television. The only decent cop show is "Law & Order."

The public thinks cops are dumb people. They don't realize that Departments look for more experienced officers. It's very competitive. Many officers are college graduates; some even attend night school to obtain their Masters Degrees. The new recruits are much better rounded. The television programs send the wrong message to the general public.

They correlate cops and donuts. People don't know what we really do. They think we do nothing and that we're uneducated. We have to take care of everybody's problems. We actually can change a person's life—their livelihood. They are under many misconceptions. In reality, John Q. Public doesn't really give a damn. They really don't care.

Public contact is negative. They only call when they have a problem. People have a warped perception of the way the laws are. Then, if you tell them something they don't want to hear, they get mad at you.

Public Perception

They think that everything is personal towards them, that we came looking specifically to find them and see if they were breaking the law. Being an officer is just a job to me. Unfortunately, nobody likes cops.

The general public thinks that cops are mean and hard. That we're supposed to be polite and courteous towards law abiding citizens and mean sons of bitches towards criminals.

The citizens believe that half the officers should be in their neighborhood, patrolling all the time. The public council doesn't understand how our police department functions. One year, we asked for five new cars and five trees (racks for the lights and sirens). They approved three new cars and five new trees. It was so stupid. Why would we need two extra racks without the cruisers to go with it? It comes down to dollars and cents, even when a large percentage of the general public has no understanding of our operation.

When people are stopped for motor vehicle violations, they tell us that we should be apprehending the "real" criminals. Firemen are considered heroes and cops are the bad guys. They think that all we want to do is pull someone over.

Public Perception

Many people think that the police profession in general is a simplistic vocation which doesn't require a great deal of aptitude. In reality, a police officer is required to have a mastery of more disciplines than perhaps any other occupation that exists. Many other people have a support staff and the luxury of time in their decision-making process, but the police officer must process the information and make the decision right then and there, without the luxury of time.

SOUNDING BOARD

This chapter covers different comments and views which the officers had expressed during the interviews. There was no specific question relating to this chapter or the responses. Whenever an officer left the topic of the questions at hand, I decided to keep on taking notes.

Many officers feel they get a "bad rap" from the public and they don't receive the support they need from the communities they have sworn to protect and serve. There is an enormous amount of frustration directed towards the prison system, as well as the courts. The officers do their jobs, arrest the criminals, and before they even finish the paperwork, the criminals are back out on the streets committing the same crimes or other crimes.

Just sit back and read what some of the officers had to say when free to express their other opinions.

> The public should realize that crime is on the rise because of the difficulties in prosecuting cases. A lot of people make references to the good old days and how it should come back. What people fail to realize is that the "good old days" law enforcement officials didn't have the restrictions today's law enforcers are facing. It seems there is so much more emphasis placed on a person's rights, than the crime that he or she committed. The pendulum has swung too far the other way. In order to correct this problem, people have got to be willing to give up rights and tighten or eliminate loop holes in the law. If not, rewrite the laws. The Constitution is taken too literally; protecting the criminals and leaving the victims feeling left out. Sure an argument can be made that giving the police more power is an invitation to abuse, but I feel this problem can be addressed and dealt with. The law enforcement officer must be given some more freedom in order to do his or her job better.

Sounding Board

As a regular law abiding citizen, you have no rights until you break the law. Then you have all the rights in the world.

Most criminals are less than animals. Animals at least protect their young. These creatures don't. They'll sacrifice their wives, girlfriends and many times their children.

The government is only open 16 hours a day. The police are the only ones that are open 24 hours a day. If anyone has a problem, they call us, day or night, and we're there.

If anyone wants welfare, all they have to do is come to Connecticut; we'll take anyone and everyone. We'll even pay you welfare under as many names you wish to use. This causes such a problem, where the people don't need to work. They hang out and do their drugs all day long. When they get bored or need more money, they just go out and commit a crime. They don't have to worry too much about going to jail for their crimes. The public defender will plead that because they have such a low self esteem and are on welfare, they couldn't be responsible for their crimes. So they get off.

People need to be more educated about what we really do for a living. We have families, too. Why do people think that we're like robots, only out there to give them a hard time? We're not. I have personal problems just like anybody else.

Sounding Board

Police are a necessary evil.

I'm now working on the ROAD plan. I'm retired on active duty.

Don't let your kid become a cop. If he wants to be a lawyer—shoot him!

If people knew how much stress there is in the Department, they might just give us a little more slack when we're out there in the community, just doing our job.

An officer goes through three different stages while working on the force: first, they're gung-ho, then they become very cynical, then they get to the point where I am—you just don't give a shit.

There's no longer the respect for the police that there was back in the early sixties.

Off duty, the younger officers hang out amongst themselves. They need to adjust to their new profession. It's a real eye opener.

Sounding Board

Why do people always have to blame me when I give them a ticket for speeding? They tell me it'll be my fault if they lose their license. As if I was the one that made them speed. People: grow up and get a life! Take responsibility for your actions.

Getting a ticket should be a learning experience—not a crucifixion. The fines are too high here in the State of Connecticut. In a lot of areas, the posted speed limits need to be more consistent. I still have to do my job, though.

Lockouts are the few positive calls I enjoy. That's when someone locked their keys in the car. I'm more than happy to help them.

Connecticut is much too liberal.

People don't understand the peer pressure put on teens to join gangs.

People need to be more responsible in the upbringing of their children. Children learn by example. If you do drugs, they'll do drugs. If you hit your spouse, they'll think it's acceptable to hit theirs when they get married.

Sounding Board

Everyone expects us to solve all their problems when we get called to a Domestic. We just do the best we can. We're not psychiatrists, although we need to be at times.

Too many people think that we're racist. We're not. We treat everyone the same way, with the same concern and courtesy.

The Miranda Law hurts the police.

There are a few bad apples within most of the Police Departments, but there is in every job.

We see the worst in people.

I hate that people take the actions of a few and automatically think that all cops are crooked or dishonest. We're not. The newspaper and media always focus on the bad things. People want to see negative, otherwise the newspapers wouldn't sell.

Towns should fight the lawsuits against the officers instead of just paying them. People are too sue-happy.

Sounding Board

Human life becomes important once the pressure groups get involved along with the State. There is so much liberalism. When drugs were just a city problem, the penalties were stiffer. Once they made their way into the suburbs, drug offenses became decriminalized from a felony to a misdemeanor.

Blame: never blame the person who did the crime. Find a government agency or someone with big shoulders to put the blame on. It's the constant "Not me, not my fault" syndrome.

Force controls, whether it's physical or economic strength. A good example was/is the Mafia. We need stricter penalties which are enforceable. We need to take the profit out of drugs and other related crimes.

It's very frustrating at times when we lack the proper equipment.

It's difficult to get good officers. We do the best we can in screening, but sometimes we make a mistake and hire someone who shouldn't be an officer. We're only human.

The public forgets that I have money and family problems just like them. We get divorced. Sometimes we do really need to have a drink once we get off duty.

People lack common sense.

There are no fines for the serious crimes. The other day all the criminal charges concerning drugs were dropped against the six defendants. The only person found guilty of a crime that day was a man that had caught too many crabs. He had to pay a hefty fine. What message does this give to the real criminals?

The police department is quasi-military. There is a chain of command. We have rules and regulations.

The public is more involved in our Department, which is good and bad. They're more critical of everything that we do. The paperwork alone is almost unbearable and the computers are complicated.

Our crime rate is very low within our town, but the public still thinks that it's higher than their expectations of a Police Department. Maybe, if we had more cooperation from the public—giving us the information we need—we could bring it down even lower.

Our court system has failed dramatically. There's no question about that fact.

Sounding Board

Crime is everyone's problem. Without the public getting involved, there will always be crimes and criminals getting away with it.

Affirmative Action has had a serious effect on the police departments. We no longer hire and promote based on knowledge and experience. It's done on quotas. There are a lot of good men and women that are more than qualified to do more than just a patrolman's job, but politics and quotas keep them from excelling. You can see it in their attitudes. It's so disheartening.

The prisons are such a joke here in Connecticut. So is our legal system.

Society needs to get back to the family values. A family isn't necessarily both parents; it's those close to you that influence your life. Responsibility starts at home.

Maybe if people understood that when we've stopped them for speeding and found they also had a child in the car that wasn't in a car seat, we're giving them a ticket not only for breaking the law, but also to make them more responsible. They're not aware of the fact that I might have just arrested a man for sexually assaulting a fourteen month old baby several hours earlier, and there they are not taking care of their own child's safety. That makes me very angry. The children are our future. So many people shouldn't have become parents; they're too irresponsible.

Sounding Board

People think that crime is someone else's problem—until it hits home. Why don't people get involved and help us to rid their neighborhoods of the drugs and crimes? Because they think it's our problem.

Sometimes my days are like a roller coaster. I help rescue a drowning child in the morning and I arrest a man for sexually assaulting his two year old niece in the afternoon. Your emotions some days just swing from one mood to the next, depending on the call or situation.

We have to make decisions in a split second. It then takes the courts months to decide if what we did was correct. We don't have the luxury of time.

We're probably the only profession that gets assaulted on a daily basis just because of the profession we've chosen.

I wish that everyone who drinks and drives could see what others have caused when they've hit an innocent person. They need to see the pain and suffering, the blood and the twisted metal. They need to see the grief when I tell the parents that their 18 year old honor student daughter was killed by a drunk driver. Maybe they'd think twice about having that one last drink or maybe they'd let someone else drive them home. Cars don't kill people—people kill people.

Sounding Board

COMMENTARY

Author's note: This section presents commentaries written by several police officers on various topics.

Frustration . . . . page 134
by an anonymous Police Officer

Who Will Wear the Badge . . . . page 138
by Col. Joseph S. Perry, Jr., Retired

Career Choice . . . . page 140
by Chief Patrick Hedge

Fear . . . . page 142
by Chief Robert A. Williams

Controversy . . . . page 144
by Chief Leroy Bangham

Commentary

FRUSTRATION
by an anonymous Police Officer

My frustration is now complete. Never did I dream I would encounter such obstacles as I have faced in the past years of police work. The obstacles I expected were to originate from the "bad guys." The largest and most stress producing obstacles I faced never pointed a gun at me or threatened to do me physical harm. If someone had told me the toughest battles would be fought within the four walls of the police department, I would have shrugged it off as a "sour grapes" comment from a cynical individual ready to retire. I have learned, first hand, there is more stress produced by those "on our side" then I ever faced on the street.

There are considerable differences between those who are employed in the private sector as managers and those who are "managers" within an area of government, whether it is at the federal level or the municipal level. The differences are readily noticeable. Private sector managers (CEO's, presidents, department heads, etc.) are aware that new and creative ideas are absolutely necessary in order to stay in business and ahead of the competition. They realize that saving money is the same as earning it. They are aware that an efficient operation is also an effective one. These concepts are incorporated within company philosophies because they know that they do not have the luxury of the bottomless pocketbook called the taxpayer to fund their businesses. Change is necessary. Progressive attitudes are a must. Attacking age-old problems with new ideas is welcomed. Government managers have a different slant when it applies to progressive attitudes. Change is challenged more vehemently by government administrators as it is perceived as failure on their part, unless of course, it enlarges their own bureaucracy. But bureaucracies do not fight crime. The working cop on the street has to fight the criminals and the bureaucrats. And guess which one is the worst foe of the two?

Administrators who fight change and progressive tactics all have the battle cry "that's the way we did it twenty years ago" or "this has been working for the past ten years; why change now?" I do not have the statistics to support the next statement but I believe that those who attain management levels in the private sector and then join a government agency bring with them the positive attitudes and progressive thinking and eventually become assets to their agencies by looking further than the end of the current fiscal year. Government employees on the other hand that make the jump to the private sector, bring with them the outdated, antiquated attitudes that are so prevalent among bureaucracies. This type of short-sighted behavior has to be eliminated if government wishes to attain more with their current budgets. Anyone handling a multi-million dollar budget has to be aware of their investments and the potential returns for a period greater than one fiscal year. Only within a government agency could ineffectiveness and inefficiency be rewarded. Only a branch of government would boast about its short-sighted, narrow minded and self serving efforts. An individual of vision who can attack an old problem in a new and creative fashion need not apply. Those who present fresh ideas are considered wave makers and boat rockers. Pass out the life vests I say.

All through your career you will be told you need to be a team player. Their definition of team goes something like this. You are on your way to being a team player if:

1. *They like you.*

    The hell with your work record, work ethic or character. "He can't write a report to save his life and has a pattern of excessive sick time but he's a hell of guy and doesn't get under my skin."

2. *You are not the subject of any controversy where the administration may be questioned about your actions or decisions.*

    Police work is fraught with controversy. A good cop, a cop doing the job he was hired to do, will be controversial. Period. That's just the way it is. Supreme Court decisions arise from cops doing their job.

3. *You agree with their (the administration or a specific administrator's) philosophies and politics.*

    Lord forbid you should disagree with either of these. One of the reasons they attained their present position has to do with politics. These people will pander to the politically correct crowd and expect you to do the same. A flip-flop of policy is the norm. They tend to do what is popular rather than what is right for all concerned.

The real killer is when they use the condescending phrase "there is no 'I' in 'T-E-A-M'." I see a lot of "I's" in "TEAM." A team is made up of *individuals* with a common goal or purpose. Each individual brings certain characteristics, talents and abilities to the team. *Initiative* is a positive and much sought after characteristic necessary for team work. A person with an *industrious* nature is an asset. The biggest "I", the most important "I" that seems to be overlooked is *integrity*. Without integrity you are nothing. Your team is nothing. Personal integrity, honesty and the refusal to compromise either is never

Commentary

considered unless, of course, they don't like you, you are controversial or you are not in lock-step with their politics. But then again, someone who changes their beliefs in order to be politically correct can't have much in the way of integrity.

Moving outside the four walls and into the state legislature, one can view the most transparent of all people; our lawmakers. Lawyers making laws. Does that seem like a conflict of interest to anybody? Built-in loopholes made by practicing attorneys. Laws so convoluted and overly complicated that successful prosecution is nearly impossible. Keep in mind that most lawyers are not involved in courtroom drama everyday like is seen on "LA Law" or "Matlock" or other attorney-based television shows. An attorney contends with lots and lots of routine, mundane, monotonous paperwork everyday. They become accustomed to an overabundance of paperwork and sometimes cannot function unless there is a mountain of forms to accompany their daily routine. So it seems natural it would carry over when creating or revising laws. Then again, many of us wonder if the extensive paperwork is created just on the chance the working cop, after a busy shift, may forget to fill in an area or check off a box on a report, thus making the arrest null. Who knows?

Our law makers are politicians first and foremost. They will create new laws and revise old laws to make them "tougher" based on the public opinion at the time. The public wants tougher laws? We'll make tougher laws so be sure to vote for us next time because we did what you wanted. Common sense apparently has no role when the legislature is in session. For example, anyone caught in possession of or selling drugs within fifteen hundred feet of a school, housing project or state-licensed and approved day care center (town approved doesn't count) is subjected to stiffer penalties than the regular drug dealer on any other street. I can stand at the school bus stop and sell drugs or stop the mothers as they bring their kids to day care and sell them drugs, and as long as I am more than fifteen hundred feet away from a school, housing project or day care center, I will not be subjected to as severe a penalty. Hell, I can ride the school bus and sell drugs to each child entering the bus and I still will not serve as stiff a sentence if I get caught, *as long as I am not within fifteen hundred feet of a school, housing project, or state-certified day care center*. According to our lawmakers, those residing in housing projects require more protection than the rest of the community. Children attending city or town certified day care centers are not protected with the same tenacity as those who attend state certified centers. How is that for a law that creates second class citizens? It seems as though our lawmakers have decided that those dealing drugs to children are bad only if they are near a specific area. The others dealing drugs to children aren't so bad, for some foolish reason only our State Representatives and Senators can comprehend.

Commentary

The lawmakers cannot shoulder all the blame for our ineffective criminal justice system. The courts have lent a hand in making it impossible to keep the worst of society off the streets, too. The United States Supreme Court recently adopted what is referred to as a "plain feel doctrine." (Minnesota v. Dickerson) When an officer conducts a pat down of the outer clothing of an individual, he is feeling for a weapon or something that may be used as a weapon. Many times during this pat down, the officer through his training and experience, can determine by touch that an object secreted in a pocket is in fact some form of narcotics. When the officer feels the object and can conclude it is narcotics, the common sense approach is to remove the item from the pocket and examine it. The "plain feel" part comes from the fact that an officer, by touch, can distinguish a weapon from other items commonly carried in a pocket and can distinguish narcotics from other items by its feel and packaging. It only makes sense to make an arrest when drugs are found rather than leave it in the pocket because it does not feel like a weapon. Has Connecticut adopted this common sense doctrine? You guessed it! An appellate court has ruled the removing of narcotics from an individual after it has been identified by touch is an illegal search and the evidence must therefore be suppressed. Let's hope the Connecticut Supreme Court rules otherwise.

Most of us can face down the bad guys no matter what they throw in our direction but we can't fight our battles on three fronts. It's not the bad guys that beat us down, it is the police administrators who constantly and consistently demonstrate regressive attitudes and refuse to accept any form of change; it is the lawmakers making complicated, nearly unenforceable laws, and when they are enforceable, prosecution is limited at best. And last, the liberal courts that worry more about the rights of the accused rather than the rights of the individual or the community. I would like to bring our lawmakers and judges to view the battered, broken and bloody body of an infant who received its fatal injuries from its crack-smoking father who couldn't stand the child's constant crying and decided to swing it around by its feet and dash its head against the floor until the child died, and see what they would have to say about the accused's rights.

Commentary

WHO WILL WEAR THE BADGE?
by Col. Joseph S. Perry, Jr., Retired
Commanding Officer Connecticut State Police

An organization is only as good as the people who work within it. In no other profession is this statement as true as in law enforcement. In policing today, complex issues surround the recruitment, selection, and training of entry level persons.

Professional law enforcement has long adhered to the process necessary to select the candidates best suited to wear the badge. The dividends gained from well-suited, well-selected, and well-trained police officers outweigh the time and expense needed to develop that officer. Professional administrators have devised comprehensive recruiting and training programs. Far beyond merely finding a body to fill the slot, recruiting takes into account such concerns as community issues, diversity, the establishment of exacting, but realistic standards, and overall fairness in the selection process. In return for this effort, a department is rewarded with a professional police officer.

Recent events will undoubtedly produce new concerns in the area of police hiring. The passage by the U.S. Congress and the recent signing into law of the Crime Bill by President William Clinton will have many police administrators rushing to hire additional personnel under the provisions of the new law. Many departments will see their staffing levels expand overnight. Unfortunately, some agencies will lose sight of the importance of standards and will concentrate on merely increasing the overall size of the department.

In the past, this rapid expansion has lead to a general lowering of standards, less than adequate applicant background investigations, and shortened recruit training periods. Much of this has occurred because the staffing increases have often gone beyond department's ability to adequately review, test, and train new applicants. Consequently, many agencies have experienced a number of ills including instances of police corruption and increased liability problems. An agency's financial setbacks caused episodes such as improper search and illegal arrests are only part of the cost. The cost of lowering standards for police candidates is measured by the loss of community standing, as well as the loss of dollars.

The availability of funding has always created a sense of urgency in the law enforcement community. Many administrators are quick to seize grant money and set off on a course of rapid, if not runaway, expansion. Clearly, it makes sense to resist the urge to immediately spend and plot a course. Today's police administrators need to review their hiring standards and stand steadfast besides those goals. The lowering of standards just to get everyone on board that the funding will cover is short-sighted. An agency's future is built on the character of each individual officer. Time and time again, police departments around the country have come to realize only too late that the lessening of standards has fostered corruption, brutality and other police misconduct.

The recruitment, selection and training of police candidates must not sacrifice quality for quantity. In a democratic society, order and justice is safeguarded by the skill of a chosen few, rather than the brute force of many. For the agency that demands quality from the persons they select to wear the badge, the agency will excel and will be viewed as a community asset and not a liability.

Commentary

Career Choice
by Chief Patrick Hedge
Stonington Police Department

Officer Alice Logan is on the evening shift in a large city and her beat is a high crime area. At about 10 P.M. she receives a radio transmission directing her to a disturbance and the dreaded words, "shots fired," emanate from the police radio. Her palms sweating, heart rate increasing and her throat suddenly dry, Alice proceeds rapidly to the scene. As she exits her patrol vehicle, her eyes dart from side to side, hoping she is not in the cross hairs of an enemy's weapon. Alice spies a small object lying on the pavement. Closer examination reveals a youthful female mortally wounded by gunshots. Alice cradles the girl's head in her arms in an attempt to comfort her and tears stream down Alice's cheeks. The girl takes her last breath. Just another routine call on a weekend evening in the city. So much for Alice's dream of becoming an officer to help people to a better life. When the shooter is found and arrested, it is discovered that he was a drug dealer trying to intimidate a poor paying customer by firing a nine millimeter handgun indiscriminately in his direction, only to take the unfulfilled life of a thirteen year old girl.

Officer John Hopkins, a member of a suburban police department responds to a domestic dispute and upon his arrival he discovers a woman bleeding and bruised at the hands of her husband who is half asleep on a sofa in the living room. Hopkins determines the evidence is sufficient to arrest the husband and he reads the intoxicated subject his rights. The battered woman standing there, wonders what her rights are and what the future holds for her. The husband explains to Officer Hopkins that his marriage vows gave him the right to beat his wife because she continually failed to obey him.

Officer Henry Johnson, one of two officers assigned the midnight shift in a small eastern town, is dispatched to a motor vehicle accident on a dark country road. The road is slightly wet from the mist and the fog covering the countryside. When he signs off, at the scene he discovers the lifeless body of a high school girl whom he recognizes as the daughter of the owner of the local pharmacy and a schoolmate of his own daughter. The victim had been thrown from the vehicle she was driving. After radioing for assistance and an ambulance, Officer Johnson checks the other vehicle involved and finds another youngster in the vehicle with minor injuries. The odor of alcohol is prevalent and the interior of the car is covered with empty beer cans.

Commentary

As a police officer, you see the worst in people. They lie, they cheat, they steal and they assault those they supposedly love. The victims have no voice but yours and the criminals fear no one but you. Few, if any of these miscreants, take responsibility for what they do. There is no other career that allows one to experience life fully, with all its pleasure and pain, and its highs and lows.

Stress on police officers is greater today than ever before. You might think the obvious reason for tension and stress is the idea that every time you put on your uniform and leave the station house or precinct, you are a target for the uncontrolled criminals in today's society. Most officers confidently deal with this fear and control it very well. They accept the unpopular role of society's conscience and perform such roles in an exemplary manner. What causes stress and frustration is operating out of substandard buildings, in court houses advocating criminals' rights and rehabilitation and ignoring the plight of under-represented victims. In their homes and community where their role is anything but appreciated, they feel betrayed by the commanders and managers of their departments who should be guiding them and protecting them and not creating a bureaucracy to protect themselves from scrutiny.

Officers are required to do more today with less. Necessary equipment requires a struggle. Potential lifesaving vests compete with textbooks for funding. Vehicles that officers would not risk their families in are assigned to them for patrol. Special interest groups try to remove the officers' guns, ammunition and other weapons because they might be used inappropriately. This is stress.

The fact that dangerous felons are apprehended at the risk of the officers' lives and beat the officers back to the streets after their court appearance. This is stress.

Criticism from the media for being brusque and insensitive and often falsely accused of brutality. This is stress.

Through all this stress and tension there are moments when a victim writes a note of thanks, a criminal gets the maximum sentence, your superior says, 'well done', and a youngster smiles and squeezes your hand in admiration. You now realize why you chose the career of police officer.

Commentary

Fear

by Chief Robert A. Williams
Suffield Police Department

Fear: Without a doubt, it is the most terrifying emotion that people will ever experience. This emotion recognizes no age, no gender, and no national origin. It is immune from classification by marital status, political affiliation, religious preference and economic class. It transcends the borders of cities, towns, and state lines. Although the effect may be "very individual" in signs, symptoms and reactions, there is no mistaking the impact it has on society.

Unique to the phenomena of fear is it's ability to come packaged in two very distinct and different forms. Fear can be the emotional reaction to a situation as it is happening. Your getting chest pains and being in fear of the heart attack that you know is happening at the moment, is very situation oriented. The far more crippling effect of fear on society comes in the second form, fear based upon what one thinks might happen.

This perception of fear has left Law Enforcement in a dilemma. As we attempt to protect and serve the people living in our cities and towns, the perception of fear has become more prevalent.

Today's news media, in every form, has done a wonderful job of insuring that the perception of fear has been reinforced on a daily basis. Their continuous reports of shootings, violence, drugs and victims has left individuals, neighborhoods and communities convinced that everything they perceived and should have reason to fear, is reality. Why are so many major American cities failing economically and losing their residents, businesses and cultural attractions? Perhaps the perception of crime and the fear that accompanies it is one of the major factors.

Perceived fear keeps people from getting involved, going out at night, or standing up for what they know is right. They translate these perceived fears into the way they raise their children, the interaction they have with their neighbors and communities and what they expect from the Law Enforcement community.

As Congress wrestled with the now infamous Crime Bill, they were really trying to address the emotion of fear into the minds of their constituents at home. People have become emotionally crippled by real and perceived fear of crimes. They want someone to do something which will at a minimum, stop things from happening, to address the activity that forms the foundation of their fear.

Commentary

Can we realistically blame anyone, after watching the evening news or reading the daily paper, for being afraid. Afraid of the schools because an eleven year old came to school with a gun, afraid of the cities because a drive-by shooting killed another child or innocent bystander, afraid of people on the street because the court rarely incarcerates anyone but the most violent of criminals. They are afraid to retake their neighborhoods from the drug dealers, prostitutes and other criminals because they have seen the body of someone else in America. The result: The news media was there to interview the grieving members of the families left behind. To those at home, this is proof that every fear they perceived is not their imaginations, it is reality in America.

Could the popularity of today's television, books and movies dealing with the police work be based upon fear? Perhaps it is the only place where people today can feel safe and watch the good guys win. This form of entertainment reaches the feelings of people that fear has suppressed.

Until those we have elected to maintain and improve the quality of life in our society are subjected to the ordinary citizen's emotion of fear, both actual and perceived, they will forever come up short in their attempts to legislate change. These politicians will profess they understand the crime problem and will surround themselves with uniformed police officers for the public record. In reality, they can't come close to understanding the ordinary citizen's fears. In a quiet moment, it is amusing to imagine a Senator without his entourage, motorcade, and aides in a policeman's uniform; imagine him working two weeks in a precinct of a major city. Put them on the street. Let them handle the calls, walk and talk the streets as just another officer. Send them to the shootings, put their hands on the bleeding and then go to the homes and tell the mothers and fathers their children are dead. Send them into a fourth floor apartment to arrest the man with the gun. Then send them back to Washington to do a Crime Bill.

A little fear real or perceived, would do one hell of a lot towards having them identify with the common person. It's a fantasy, but it ranks right up there with watching the cops solve a murder, arrest the bad guy and having the judge send him to prison for life, all within a half-hour television show.

Until our elected officials and judges have walked the real streets and have experienced the emotion called fear, don't look for much to change. Their reality and yours are worlds apart.

Commentary

Controversy
by Chief Leroy Bangham
Farmington Police Department

When I was asked to write some comments by the author of this book, I asked her why she chose me, when there are many Chiefs of Police in Connecticut. She informed me that her reason revolved around the fact that a number of people during her research had mentioned me as a controversial Chief of Police.

I don't deny the fact that my reputation is as the author describes. I also don't do anything that would discourage such a description. I would like my comments in this book to look at why I've earned such a reputation.

Do I advocate extreme positions? Do I or my Department practice radical police procedures? Do all other police professionals disagree with me? The answer to all these questions is "No."

What causes a Chief of Police to be described as controversial is his or her willingness to speak up for what they believe to be true. For some reason, the law enforcement profession is suspicious of anyone willing to speak their mind. It rarely matters that a person is right or that a particular issue should be debated. It only matters that a person has the gall to challenge the status quo.

The only way that any profession can remain viable and useful to society is to constantly look at itself and challenge its way of operating. This should be done by people inside the profession. Look at the medical profession or the field of law. These professions are constantly evaluating their procedures, ethics and methods. I don't hear the word controversial and they continue to grow and improve.

Law enforcement has a direct impact on the quality of life of our citizens. We must change. If we are to survive, we must stop branding the advocates of change as controversial and actually look at what they are saying.

MUNICIPAL POLICE DIRECTORY

Ansonia Police Department, Chief James J. McGrath
2 Elm Street, Ansonia, CT 06401, (203)735-1885

Avon Police Department, Chief James A. Martino, Jr.
60 West Main Street, Avon, CT 06001, (860)677-9746

Berlin Police Department, Chief Gerald R. Charmut
240 Kensington Road, Kensington, CT 06037, (860)828-7080

Bethel Police Department, Acting Chief James P. O'Hara
49 Plum Trees Road, Bethel, CT 06801, (203)744-7900

Bloomfield Police Department, Captain Richard Mulhall
785 Park Avenue, Bloomfield, CT 06002, (860)242-5501

Branford Police Department, Chief William F. Holohan
33 Laurel Street, Avenue, Branford, CT 06405, (203)481-4241

Bridgeport Police Department, Supt. Thomas J. Sweeney
300 Congress Street, Bridgeport, CT 06604, (203)576-7601

Bristol Police Department, Chief John DiVenere
131 North Main Street, Bristol, CT 06010, (860)584-7931

Brookfield Police Department, Chief John W. Anderson
63 Silvermine Road, Brookfield, CT 06804, (203)775-2576

Canton Police Department, Chief Lowell F. Humphrey
4 Market Street, Collinsville, CT 06022-0168, (860)693-0221

Cheshire Police Department, Chief George R. Merriam
500 Highland Avenue, Cheshire, CT 06410 (860)271-5500

Chester Police Department, Off. in Chg. Lt. Ken Reid
65 Main Street, Chester, CT 06412 (860)526-3605

Clinton Police Department, Chief Joseph P. Faughnan
48 East Main Street, Clinton, CT 06413, (860)669-0451

Municipal Police Directory

Coventry Police Department, Chief Frank V. Trzaskos
1712 Main Street, Coventry, CT 06238, (860)742-7331

Cromwell Police Department, Chief Anthony J. Salvatore
5 West Street, Cromwell, CT 06416, (860)635-2256

Danbury Police Department, Chief Nelson F. Macedo
120 Main Street, Danbury, CT 06810, (203)797-4611

Darien Police Department, Chief Hugh McManus
Hecker Avenue, Darien, CT 06820, (203)655-9239

Derby Police Department, Chief Andrew Cota
125 Water Street, Derby, CT 06418, (203)734-1651

East Hampton Police Department, Chief Eugene B. Rame
20 East High Street, East Hampton, CT 06424, (860)267-9544

East Hartford Police Department, Chief James Shay
497 Tolland Street, East Hartford, CT 06108, (860)528-4401

East Haven Police Department, Chief James C. Criscuolo
471 North High Street, East Haven, CT 06512, (203)468-3820

East Lyme Police Department, Chief David Cini
Pennsylvania Avenue, East Lyme, CT 06357, (860)739-5900

Easton Police Department, Chief John F. Solomon
225 Center Road, Easton, CT 06612, (203)268-4111

East Windsor Police Department, Chief Thomas J. Laufer, Sr.
25 School Street, East Windsor, CT 06088, (860)627-9371

Enfield Police Department, Chief Ronald D. Marcotte, Sr.
293 Elm Street, Enfield, CT 06082, (860)763-6400

Fairfield Police Department, Chief Ronald T. Sullivan
100 Reef Road, Fairfield, CT 06430, (203)254-3312

Farmington Police Department, Chief LeRoy Bangham
1 Monteith Drive, Farmington, CT 06034, (860)673-8216

Glastonbury Police Department, Chief James M. Thomas
2108 Main Street, P. O. Box 535, Glastonbury, CT 06033, (860)633-8301

Granby Police Department, Chief Jeremiah P. Marron, Sr.
15 North Granby Road, Granby, CT 06035, (860)653-7221

Greenwich Police Department, Chief Kenneth J. Moughty
11 Bruce Place, Greenwich, CT 06836, (203)622-8000

Groton Police Department (town), Chief David Vanasse
68 Groton Long Point Road, Groton, CT 06340, (860)445-9721

Groton Police Department (city), Chief Wilfred J. Blanchette, Jr.
295 Meridan Street, Groton, CT 06340, (860)445-2451

Groton Long Point Police Department, Chief George A. White
46 Beach Road, Groton, CT 06340, (860)536-4921

Guilford Police Department, Chief Kenneth R. Cruz
400 Church Street, Guilford, CT 06437, (203)453-8489

Hamden Police Department, Chief John P. Ambrogio
2900 Dixwell Avenue, Hamden, CT 06518, (203)230-4000

Hartford Police Department, Chief Joseph Croughwell
50 Jennings Road, Hartford, CT 06120, (860)527-6300

Madison Police Department, Chief James Cameron
8 Old Route 79, Madison, CT 06443-2342, (203)245-2721

Manchester Police Department, Chief Henry Minor
239 East Middle Turnpike, Manchester, CT 06040, (860)645-5500

Marlborough Police Department, Off. in Chg. Tpr. Jeffery Megin
26 North Main Street, Marlborough, CT 06447, (860)295-9098

Meriden Police Department, Chief Robert E. Kosienski
50 West Main Street, Meriden, CT 06451, (203)238-1911

Middlebury Police Department, Chief Patrick J. Bona
200 Southford Road, Middlebury, CT 06762, (203)577-4028

Municipal Police Directory

Middletown Police Department, Chief George R. Aylward
66 Church Street, Middletown, CT 06457, (860)347-6941

Milford Police Department, Chief Thomas E. Flaherty
430 Boston Post Road, Milford, CT 06460, (203)878-6551

Monroe Police Department, Chief Robert J. Wesche, Sr.
7 Fan Hill Road, Monroe, CT 06468, (203)261-3622

Naugatuck Police Department, Chief Dennis Clisham
211 Spring Street, Naugatuck, CT 06770, (203)729-5221

New Britain Police Department, Chief William Sencio
125 Columbus Boulevard, New Britain, CT 06051, (860)229-0321

New Canaan Police Department, Chief Erik Damm
174 South Avenue, New Canaan, CT 06840, (203)966-2626

New Haven Police Department, Chief Melvin Wearing
1 Union Avenue, New Haven, CT 06519, (203)946-6316

Newington Police Department, Chief Richard Klett
131 Cedar Street, Newington, CT 06111, (860)666-8445

New London Police Department, Chief Bruce Rinhart
5 Governor Winthrop Blvd., New London, CT 06320, (860)447-5269

New Milford Police Department, Chief James Sweeney
49 Poplar Street, New Milford, CT 06776, (203)355-3133

Newtown Police Department, Chief James Lysaght
3 Main Street, Newtown, CT 06470, (203)426-5841

North Branford Police Department, Chief Mathew L. Canelli
PO Box 301, North Branford, CT 06475, (203)484-2703

North Haven Police Department, Chief Kevin Connolly
260 Forest Road, North Haven, CT 06473, (203)239-5321

Norwalk Police Department, Chief Harry Rilling
297 West Avenue, Norwalk, CT 06852, (203)854-3000

Municipal Police Directory

Norwich Police Department, Chief Louis Fusaro
70 Thames Street, Norwich, CT 06360, (860)886-5561

Old Saybrook Police Department, Chief Edmund H. Mosca
225 Main Street, Old Saybrook, CT 06475, (860)395-3142

Orange Police Department, Chief Edward Delaney
314 Lambert Road, Orange, CT 06477, (203)891-2130

Plainfield Police Department, Chief Gary L. Sousa
210 Norwich Road, Plainfield, CT 06374, (860)564-0804

Plainville Police Department, Chief Daniel J. Coppinger
1 Central Square, Plainville, CT 06062, (860)747-1616

Plymouth Police Department, Chief David A. Damon
80 Main Street, Terryville, CT 06786-0034, (860)589-7779

Portland Police Department, Off. in Chg. Tpr. Earl Rozman
634 Main Street, Portland, CT 06480, (860)342-6780

Prospect Police Department, Off. in Chg. TFC J. Paul Vance
12 Center Street, Prospect, CT 06712, (203)758-6150

Putnam Police Department, Chief Edward J. Perron
189 Church Street, Putnam, CT 06260, (860)928-6565

Ridgefield Police Department, Chief Thomas J. Rotunda
76 East Ridge , Ridgefield, CT 06877, (203)438-6531

Rocky Hill Police Department, Chief George Marinelli
699 Old Main Street, Rocky Hill, CT 06067, (860)258-7640

Seymour Police Department, Chief Michael Metzler
4 Wakeley Street, Seymour, CT 06483, (203)888-2525

Shelton Police Department, Chief Robert E. White
85 Wheeler Street, Shelton, CT 06484, (203)924-1544

Simsbury Police Department, Chief Alfred L. Shull
933 Hopmeadow Street, Simsbury, CT 06070, (860)658-3100

Municipal Police Directory

Southbury Police Department, Off. In Chg. Tpr. Thomas Begert
421 Main Street South, Southbury, CT 06488, (203)264-5912

Southington Police Department, Chief William Perry
351 Main Street, Southington, CT 06489, (860)621-0101

South Windsor Police Department, Chief Gary K. Tyler
151 Sand Hill Road, South Windsor, CT 06074, (860)644-2551

Stamford Police Department, Chief G. Patrick Tully
805 Bedford Street, Stamford, CT 06901, (203)977-4444

Stonington Police Department, Chief Patrick F. Hedge
166 South Broad Street, Pawcatuck, CT 06379, (860)599-4411

Stratford Police Department, Chief Robert E. Mossman
900 Longbrook Avenue, Stratford, CT 0 6497, (203)385-4100

Suffield Police Department, Chief Robert A. Williams
911 Mountain Road, Suffield, CT 06078, (860)668-3870

Thomaston Police Department, Chief Edward T. Grabherr
158 Main Street, Thomaston, CT 06787, (860)283-4343

Torrington Police Department, Chief Mahlon C. Sabo
576 Main Street, Torrington, CT 06790, (860)489-2000

Trumbull Police Department, Chief Theodore J. Amborsini
158 Edison Road, Trumbull, CT 06611, (203)261-3665

Vernon Police Department, Chief Rudolf Rossmy
725 Hartford Turnpike, Vernon, CT 06066, (860)872-9126

Wallingford Police Department, Chief Douglas L. Dortenzio
135 North Main Street, Wallingford, CT 06492, (203)294-2800

Waterbury Police Department, Supt. Edward D. Flaherty
255 East Main Street, Waterbury, CT 06702, (203)574-6911

Waterford Police Department, Chief Murray J. Pendleton
41 Avery Lane, Waterford, CT 06385, (860)442-9451

Municipal Police Directory

Watertown Police Department, Chief John F. Carroll
195 French Street, Watertown, CT 06795, (860)945-5200

West Hartford Police Department, Chief James J. Strillacci
103 Raymond Road, West Hartford, CT 06107, (860)523-5203

West Haven Police Department, Chief Michael J. Kelly
355 Main Street, West Haven, CT 06516, (203)937-3900

Weston Police Department, Chief Anthony Land
PO Box 1182, Weston, CT 06883, (203)222-2666

Westport Police Department, Chief William J. Chiarenzelli
50 Jesup Road, Westport, CT 06880, (203)227-4145

Wethersfield Police Department, Chief John S. Karangekis
505 Silas Deane Highway, Wethersfield, CT 06109, (860)721-2900

Willimantic Police Department, Chief Milton J. King
22 Meadow Street, Willimantic, CT 06226, (860)423-4541

Wilton Police Department, Chief Angelo A. Toscano
240 Danbury Road, Wilton, CT 06897, (203)834-6260

Windsor Police Department, Chief Kevin C. Searles
340 Bloomfield Avenue, Windsor, CT 06095, (860)688-5273

Windsor Locks Police Department, Chief William Gifford
4 Volunteer Drive, Windsor Locks, CT 06096, (860)627-1461

Winsted Police Department, Chief Anthony Paige
338 Main Street, Winsted, CT 06098, (860)379-2721

Wolcott Police Department, Chief James Watson, Sr.
225 Nichols Road, Wolcott, CT 06716, (203)879-1414

Woodbridge Police Department, Chief Dennis Phipps
4 Meetinghouse Lane, Woodbridge, CT 06525, (203)387-2511

Municipal Police Directory

STATE POLICE DIRECTORY

Connecticut State Police, Acting Commanding Officer, Lt. Col. Wlliam T. McGuire

Troop A—Southbury, Lt. James Salzo
90 Lakeside Road, Southbury, CT 06488, (860)566-7492

Troop B—North Canaan
Route 7, North Canaan, CT 06108, (860)238-6093

Troop C—Tolland, Lt. Louis Lacaprucia
1320 Tolland Stage Road, Tolland, CT 06084, (860)870-9500

Troop D—Danielson, Lt. Vincent McSweeney
Westcott Road, Danielson, CT 06239, (860)566-4666

Troop E—Uncasville, Lt. Thomas Snyder
PO Box 306, Uncasville, CT 06382, (860)566-4468

Troop F—Westbrook, Lt. Clifford M'Sadoques
Conn. Turnpike West, P.O. Drawer F, Westbrook, CT 06498, (860)566-4527

Troop G—Bridgeport, Lt. Peter Warren
149 Prospect Street, Bridgeport, CT 06604, (800)575-6330

Troop H—Hartford, Lt. Michael Woodson
100 Washington Street, Hartford, CT 06106, (860)541-3500

Troop I—Bethany, Lt. Edmund Brunt
631 Amity Road, Bethany, CT 06525, (203)393-4200

Troop K—Colchester
Hartford Road, Colchester, CT 06415, (860)566-4015

Troop L—Litchfield, Lt. Ben Pagoni
452B Bantam Road (Rte. 202), Litchfield, CT 06759, (860)566-7490

Troop W—Windsor Locks, Lt. Roy Beavers
Bradley International Airport, Windsor Locks, CT 06096, (860)566-7833

DISTRICT HEADQUARTERS

Central
294 Colony Street, Meriden, CT 06450, (860)238-6191

Western — **Captain Manfred Brideau**
452 Bantam Road, Litchfield, CT 06759, (860)566-4440

Eastern — **Captain Richard Wheeler**
401 West Thames Street, Unit 501, Norwich, CT 06360, (860)238-6025